HUB CULTURE

HUB CULTURE
The Next Wave of Urban Consumers

Stan Stalnaker

John Wiley & Sons (Asia) Pte Ltd

■ Other Wiley Editorial Offices:
John Wiley & Sons, Inc., 605 Third Avenue, New York, NY 10158-0012, USA
John Wiley & Sons Ltd, Baffins Lane, Chichester, West Sussex PO19 1UD, England
John Wiley & Sons (Canada) Ltd, 22 Worcester Road, Rexdale, Ontario M9W 1L1, Canada
John Wiley & Sons Australia Ltd, 33 Park Road (PO Box 1226), Milton, Queensland 4064, Australia
Wiley – VCH, Pappelallee 3, 69469 Weinheim, Germany

■ Library of Congress Cataloging in Publication Data
ISBN 0-470-82072-1

Typeset in 11/14 points, Dutch 801 by Paul Lim.
Printed in Singapore by Saik Wah Press Pte Ltd.
10 9 8 7 6 5 4 3 2 1

What once took months to accomplish
now takes seconds.
Borders, imagined and real,
at least in some information arenas,
are now non-existent.
A seamless transfer of information
takes seconds.
The challenge now is making sense
of that information,
managing it and putting it to good use.
Information is useless unless it can
make us richer, wiser or quicker.

Katherine Oliver

Contents

Prologue

I've set out to explain a way of living that has taken root in many of the world's largest cities in an attempt to help marketers understand the new motivating factors for global brand development. The central tenet of this view is that a hub-centric strategy is critical in reaching today's affluent urban populations. The view is also popping up everywhere – the realization that city life has become its own unique culture, comparable around the world in the great urban hubs. Within these hubs, there is a culture that is unique to itself but widely spread across major cities. It draws from global influences that extend far beyond nationalism.

Because so much of what we think is drawn from the cacophony of our surroundings, many things I've written about or provided as examples are increasingly being cited in other areas – from magazines to books to TV interviews. In that sense, I do not pretend that much of this is radical or new or particularly fresh. But hopefully the perspective is of use and you will find some new and usable points within these pages.

The book is centered around three ideas that define hub culture:

[1] Travel and communication are poles around which the hub lives.

[2] The hub culture is motivated by three lifestyle factors: work, leisure and relationships.

[3] The hub culture has a number of identifying factors to which

branding efforts can be linked. These include proximity, anonymity, culture adoption, biculturalism, reliance on word of mouth, experience addiction, and the acceptance and disposal of trends with studied ambivalence.

The way I've expressed this has been to tell the stories of hub people themselves, with some examples of successful projects targeted at the group. High value add goods and services seem to be the most suited for and successful with the hubs, and for that reason I tend to focus on examples from those categories. All together, I hope it is of interest. Since many of the examples are of people I know personally, I take this opportunity to thank them for sharing their thoughts and experiences with me, however accidentally. It's safe to assume where people are mentioned by first name only the name has been changed. The facts remain, but I chose to protect their identity because some issues are a little sensitive, especially to larger companies. Finally, a special word of thanks to those e-mail writers whose missives have become public property, forwarded without end through the vast network we call cyberspace – a cultural dimension where the hub spends much of its time.

Stan Stalnaker, July 2002, Hong Kong

Acknowledgments

This book would not have been possible without the following people, whom I would like to thank for providing the foundations of my understanding of global urbanism: Andrew Butcher, Jeff Casserly, Nancy Carter, Rich & Karen Jennings, Elizabeth Jennings, John Marcom, Joe & Anna Niesley, Steve & Joan Schnell, Nadine Schnell, and my fantastic family. David Sharp, formerly of John Wiley & Sons and my editors CJ Hwu and Malar Manoharan of John Wiley & Sons, were enormously helpful in motivating me to start on Hub Culture and helped guide the book in the editing phase. John McClellan at Haldanes made sure I got the best arrangements and helped me think about the big picture. Special thanks also to Mike Edie and Ed Bean on technical development of the first extensions to the project on the web and in video.

And to my friends who have been listening to me rant for months, a big thank you: Jennifer Floyd, Rebecca Kloss, Kathryn Murdoch, David Packman and Erin Stalnaker for the hours of tedious listening and for reading it early, offering your point of view, comments and criticisms. To Terry McDevitt for making me write the first sentence. Scott Barnes, Dominique Freiche, Nichole Garnaut, Jennifer Glass, Bill Powell and Christian Rowell for motivating the middle. To Rik Kirkland and Robert Friedman at FORTUNE for reviewing at last. Thanks.

chapter**one**

The New Composite

It's Sunday afternoon.

Down a quiet, tree-lined street in a forested enclave outside of Manchester, New Hampshire, lies a cultural landmark of significance to the new global urban culture. Here, sheltered among towering acorn trees in an otherwise nondescript, affluent neighborhood, is the Zimmerman House. Designed and built in 1950, it is the only Frank Lloyd Wright-designed private house open to the public in New England. The grounds are manicured and hallow in a way that few public places ever are, and the stillness that surrounds the house is palpable.

Getting here is not a simple matter of navigating a map. New Hampshire's Currier Gallery of Art, which maintains the residence and operates tours through the house, does not publicize the address of the Zimmerman House. Instead, guests are expected to rock up to the gallery in Manchester, where a modest $15 fee is garnered for a van to transport you to the actual location. The gallery people are sweet in that New England, slightly snobby blue-blood sort of way, where they only slightly look down their nose at the urban hordes that tramp through their beloved Manchester in search of the grails of modern US life: peace, nature, homemade honey and outlet malls.

When enough people have gathered to await transport to the "secret" location, it becomes evident that this sort of attraction gathers a particular segment of the broader population: young to middle-aged singles and couples with no kids and a six-figure salary, along with a few silver-coifed antique-dealer types who look like they probably knew Wright personally (why do they all have facelifts?). It is an eclectic group by any standard and one that is not defined by any obvious common trait – they are young and old, singles and couples, hip and not so groovy. But they do have one thing in common: none of them live anywhere near Manchester, and the idea of visiting this icon of suburbia has a certain whiff of pilgrimage that makes everybody a bit giggly.

Standing around, casually checking out the scene, are Ruben and Rebecca. Both are in town for the weekend and have just met, at the wedding of a mutual friend, Dana. The evening before Rebecca was seated next to Ruben at the rehearsal dinner and they hit it off right away when Ruben began talking about his exploits in Slovakia, his temporary home. This piqued Rebecca's interest, for she had spent two years in Africa, followed by a short six months in Hong Kong, from where she had just returned. Both were small town suburban American kids, who discovered that to be "successful" they would need to get as far away from home as possible.

Soon it's time to roll, and a white haired New York City transplant with a pot belly steps up and orders everybody into the Currier Gallery of Art van, complete with step assists. He drives north through the mapled streets of the town, slicing cleanly through the dappled sunlight that speckles the narrow road amid the leaves of innumerable trees along the way. A few cars trail behind, full of the 20-something city folk who wouldn't be caught dead riding in a white step-assist van. It's all so very nice and blissful.

One of those cars, of course, contains Ruben and Rebecca, who have in the course of 24 hours discovered that they share a similar philosophy toward the modern world – one that is grounded on freedom but tempered by responsibility, amid a vague disillusionment with the expectation that they should be entrepreneurs and work 20 hours a day or that they should get a job with JPChaseMorganCiti whatever and spend the next 10 years slicing foie gras at business dinners wondering when the next group restructuring will put them out on the compost heap.

Nevertheless, Ruben has already been accepted to law school, the next chapter after his two-year Slovakia stint with the Peace Corps, "trying to give something back" (but really because he was bored with consulting and wanted to do something a bit different). Rebecca, a casualty of the economic slowdown, has somehow managed to land a job selling broadband space to corporations across the US, meaning that her frequent flyer miles are ticking up much faster than the speedometer on the van in front of them ever will. This, she thinks regularly to herself, will allow at least two trips to

New York before Christmas and a good chance of attending her friends' New Year bash in Paris.

Young and cynical, affluent but cash poor, they are at a nice moment in life – experienced enough to know it's the same everywhere but still curious to want to know what else there is. They are consumed by the quest for experience.

They drive on and look out the windows with a wispy sigh, allowing themselves to miss the simplicity of these little streets and manicured houses and big red mailboxes. They shudder at the sights and say, "Can you believe it, it's so cool here" then recoil inside at the thought of being stuck here for more than another day or two. "What would you do?" is invariably the next statement. And the wonderment fades.

Eventually, after twists and turns and stop signs that lead to increasingly larger homes on increasingly greener hills, the driver slows and negotiates a big slow left into the grounds, past a plaque that reads 223 Heather Street. Here, hidden from the road by grand shrubbery and the strong tall oaks of the area, lies the home, set at a corner angle to the street: long, low and lean; languid against the demands of space that constrain it. It is classic Wright, and the first sight of the Zimmerman House imbues the viewer with a sense of Eastern serenity that comes with the recognition and active courting of balance, a Wright trait.

It is completely preserved in the style of the era in which it was built. Strikingly modern and incredibly retro at the same time, it is a snapshot of time; frozen at the moment that modern style and the urban minimalist aesthetic were born. Basically, it's *Wallpaper**'s Bethlehem.

A narrow path winds around the perimeter of the grounds, affording nicely planned views of the house. Midway through the walk, a small detour takes you past a marker of the remains of the Zimmermans themselves, neatly situated under an acorn tree that looks all the stronger for it. Gaze back toward the house from this vantage point, and the sheer beauty of Wright's work becomes evident.

Neatly balanced, the view is clean and simple: natural materials in harmony with the space around it, juxtaposed with sheer glass that reflects the afternoon sun onto a broad lawn of impossibly bright green summer grass. The world suddenly slows to a creeping walk, and it could just as easily be 1950 or 2020 – the feeling is eternal. The birds twitter and a squirrel darts in front of you, following a friend who pecks around the lawn for brown acorns, scampering up, flat against the big trees to your left. It is nature, tranquility, peace. And you think, "This is what the suburbs were supposed to be, this is why our parents moved to the suburbs, for this ideal."

And then you realize that this suburban ideal, so fresh and vibrant in 1950 at the start of the great American suburban era, is not the reality of what we got. The reality of what the suburbs became, and the general monotony that they eventually came to symbolize, are the driving force behind a generational shift toward the leading urban hubs in America – New York, Washington D.C., San Francisco and Miami – "some place with personality." The grandchildren of the Wright era (people like Ruben and Rebecca) are moving to these urban centers, and ones much farther afield, with hardly a look back, because the suburbs are becoming the new ghetto. The transformation has become so pivotal, so complete, in the great migration back to city centers, that a large enough population is now sufficiently insulated from the suburban life to be collectively nostalgic for it. This is why the urbanistas who make up the group standing around on this perfect lawn relish this Wright moment, seeking to finally understand what they were getting at when they built towns like Loma Linda and Waterford and Tyson's Corner.

In the same way The Metropolitan Museum of Art has preserved the aura of "culture that was," distilled and polished and nicely presented behind a glass case, the Wright house is a 3-D snapshot of the suburbs we always wanted: a post-modern museum of the suburban utopian ideal. We are finally far enough past modernism and the idea of a suburban ideal to look back on it with a kind of distant nostalgia, a fondness that comes with forgetting.

The Wright promise of suburban bliss has long since been lost in the cookie-cutter of corporate and city planning development, which loudly borrows from Wright, but falls short of his ideal: tranquil spaces uniquely suited to their surroundings, borrowing from the natural elements that make up the immediate vicinity. Of course, every marketing brochure for every Del Webb development in the world will deny this, but any window seat on American Airlines will quietly confirm it, with mile after mile of cul-de-sacs and pitched roofs fanning out from highway arteries on the approach through the outskirts of any significant metropolitan area. It is so depressingly similar, featuring the same Circle Ks and Home Depots and Taco Bells.

With almost 280 million Americans out there, someone has to live in these clusters of development, but the anonymity and boredom of it all can be stifling, which is why Ruben bolted to Slovakia and Rebecca decamped to the heart of Africa. Anything interesting. And after that, they both go straight to a hub city – the only place they can envision living, having left.

It used to be that society considered the city a place of anonymity and the smaller towns and cities places of measure and visibility, if only local. Today, largely driven by technology and the greater mobility that all industrialized populations enjoy, the opposite is increasingly true – the suburbs and other places are becoming anonymous, while the hubs offer visibility, and increasingly, identity.

Which is why, even if you do live in one of those cookie-cutter cities in a cookie-cutter cul-de-sac, the lure, the interest and the draw are increasingly the hub, the closest urban center. And as more kids who grew up "out there" discover "in here" the centrifugal force inward to the hubs will only grow in cultural power and influence, sucking even more life and interest out of the other areas. That's good news for inner-city real estate and the industrial bar scene, bad news for your suburban shop owner and your bored, no drivers-license-owning, crystal-meth-smoking teenager. It is intellectual feudalism, but it is market driven. It is true in degrees from the smallest to the biggest, but the power is to a few kings.

The flip side to the lure of the hubs is that they increasingly need to export their brand of living, of style, of selling, to markets outside their own center. From the dawn of the Wright era, into the '50s, '60s, '70s and '80s (even well into the '90s), that export was to these ever-expanding suburban universes, which gave them a certain quality of power, and in their own way, influence. No longer. In new-millennium America, instead of that market being the suburbs and its attendant discount malls, companies are realizing that a far more lucrative market for today's high-value goods is not the mass suburbs but the other hubs, in Europe and especially in Asia. Thus, Singapore, Tokyo and London become more important priorities than Detroit, Charleston and Denver.

As transportation costs drop and advertising and media globalize, it is becoming more lucrative and less expensive to export the ideas and products of one hub to other hubs, where at least the people are similarly with it, where ideas have shorter life cycles, and where the pace of change dictates that ideas in the subculture are rapidly assumed into the mainstream. From here they filter out to equivalent parallel markets, and downstream, the outlying mass areas that now surround all the hubs around the world.

For different reasons, the pull is drawing populations to major hubs everywhere, not just the US. Outside the US, the pull is strong and getting stronger, and the power and influence of today's major urban hubs are growing to such an extent that many of the largest have eclipsed their entire country in terms of economic performance, influence and their role in the global community. When CEOs sit at economic conferences and talk about a multipolar world and emerging markets, they don't mean countries: they mean cities. And the cities, much like during another great period of cultural transformation, the Renaissance, are driving change and innovation in a way unlike anything seen before. The city-state is on the rise again, and more than the nation, is a function of the move to more complete market economies.

What makes a hub a hub? Size is a key factor; there must be enough weight to the urban center to make it a player on the world stage. And it must contain its own brand of creative imprint – vibrant neighborhoods and ethnicity – that are unique in terms of geography, but which share a common feel to other cities around the world, bound together by the commonality of their creative uniqueness and attractiveness as a destination for visitors. These neighborhoods are key to where the people who make up hub culture gather.

At large, major hubs are more connected to each other and share a more similar culture than they do with the country in which they are located, and though they all have very different base cultures, they tend to be so mixed these days that the ethnic makeup and flavor of any of them are basically just a matter of degrees: a little heavier on this and a bit lighter on that, but overall, justified by and operating on the same guidelines, with the same people moving between them, fertilizing and connecting them into a common hybrid culture that draws from all, but is dominated by its own sheer force. Like the layers of an onion, when one sees the hubs as its own common and unique culture, new rings and layers appear. Chief among these, from a marketing view, is a new group we will call the hub influentials – the 10% of those populations that are defining the common culture and the attitude and what's hot and what's not. It is this 10% that a successful global marketer must first reach, influence and convince.

It is this whole world view on a unique culture that marketers need to be aware of: first that it exists, and second to understand how important it is for disseminating trends and products to the rest of the consumer markets. By reaching the people who define hub culture, it is possible to set in motion a ripple effect, carrying your brand with it. In addition, they are a valuable, heretofore disparate market, that when unified not by geographic location but by their hub identity, become a market force in and of themselves.

<It's Tuesday evening>
Lillian and her friends simply can't get a table anyplace. First they tried the noodle shop, then the patio at the Irish pub, before stopping for a beer at Luna's, where they still couldn't get a table. Her three friends are getting grumpy, and she's annoyed. But look around. She's amazed that a few cobbled streets can hold 20 restaurants, a park, two soaring office buildings and such sexy, cosmopolitan people. Two years ago this whole neighborhood was nothing but a mess of concrete with scaffolding and holes and pipes. And a year before that? Housing. Dilapidated, dirty and squalid.

Not that she was here then, because Lillian's experience in this place only goes back two years, and in that time she has seen a transformation in herself and her city that has been nothing short of fantastic – a transformation at least as amazing as Maria Shriver's stylist working 20 minutes before the on-air sign lights up the studio. A transformation amazing in its ability to change the slightly horrendous into the supremely beautiful: the rebirth of Shanghai, China's hub city.

On the surface, Lillian is quite different from her counterparts, Ruben and Rebecca touring the Wright house in New Hampshire. But she is part of the same emerging culture and her future identity is more closely linked with Ruben and Rebecca than with her city of birth and the people who populate her old surroundings. Her new identity in Shanghai is being shaped by her assimilation into the city, and Shanghai itself is being shaped by its assimilation into the global community, colored by an optimism born of Shanghai's skyrocketing stature among hub cities.

Lillian is lucky in that she speaks Shanghainese. This gives her an advantage over the thousands who speak different dialects, having moved to Shanghai from provinces across China over the last 10 years, seeking something of the miracle that everyone in China has heard about: how you can earn 10 times more than in your local village state-run job, how education is available and how you can be exposed to the outside world, which has swiftly moved in to take advantage of the growth happening in Shanghai. Lillian speaks some English but not much, and even though she works for a German company, her German is zero.

Lillian settles her Louis Vuitton shoulder bag onto a ledge and pouts at the host in T8 as she tries to negotiate a table. Underneath her Prada heels, which click impatiently on a wooden footbridge, a small rivulet of water runs along a stone bed, collecting in a pool where giant goldfish flit around and chase each other in a laconic stupor. Some money was spent doing up this place. Behind her, foggy glass meets handcut Indian shale floors, carefully laid to match the grains of the shale. Big banana leaves and other tropical plants cascade around the host's computer, where a sophisticated reservation and booking software shows that Lillian will have to stand a while longer, pout or no pout. Through the shadowed curtains of the reception, her friends peek into the restaurant, where groups of suitably glamorous patrons pick at food and share laughs over ice buckets holding bottles of Veuve Clicquot and Cloudy Bay. And they long. They long to share the moment, to be seen enjoying the evening with their friends when the next group comes and clicks THEIR heels at the door, peeking impatiently inside. It is, after all, the place to be scene and to be seen.

The food at T8 is "nousian" – a rather advanced form of fusion cuisine that is Asian-led as opposed to Western-led. Asian interpretations of Western cuisines, with delectable results. The restaurant virtually screams out the ideals of hub culture, for it was built for and caters to it. It is a mix of many cultures and influences, all drawn together to form a new, evolved statement that is distinctly … nothing. Or everything, depending on how you look at it. China is quickly becoming a great place for this kind of expression, but other places are adept at it as well: Sydney, the new areas of Budapest, Cape Town, Paris, it's everywhere. But in new China more completely. The décor in T8 is Japanese, but the steaks are Australian Angus. The water is French, the wines Chilean and South African (and from a number of other places). The plates are in the Thai style and the starters are Latin in flavor. Nothing is taken for proof of "foreignness" or "exoticness" but for the pure value of its contribution to the overall evolved aesthetic. The effect is sufficiently global, yet relaxed. It is purely evocative of the people who frequent it, whether it is in Shanghai or Santa Monica. Like most places of its ilk, it is also comfortably expensive, adding to the overall lure.

T8's cousins, cut of the same cloth, could be Vong in Hong Kong, New York or Chicago, or in London I-Thai at the Hempel, which inspire visions of a connected consciousness that expresses itself the same way regardless of the city in which it is found. And as the people move from this place to that and do business here and there, it all becomes "zen-blend", and you soon realize that whether you are in Shanghai or London or Bangkok, this culture is the same. And there are Lillians in all of these places, with the same identical bags and the same pouts and the same strategies to get their table, to look good, to be a success, and some of those Lillians are not even Chinese.

A lot of ink has been spilled talking about "globalization" and this certain intellectual unease that comes with the blending of all these disparate cultures and identities into one menu of combined sushi and taco platters. Critics decry the loss of humanity and breadth of experience that this so caustically entails, they bemoan the idea as if it were something avoidable, or changeable. And most of all they protest that it is cultural hegemony; that the West, or often specifically America, is responsible for this shift in tastes. But the truth is that no one country, race, or culture owns the new global aesthetic. It is definitely not American, for America is but one little piece of a much larger world view that the people who populate this lifestyle embrace.

This culture is about taking the good things that you see and using them, modifying them to fit your life and leaving out what you don't like. It's about having your manicurist in Beverly Hills try out her newly discovered Chinese traditional medicines on your nails, and chowing down on kangaroo tacos laced with wasabi. About being a Dane in London, celebrating a Kris Kringle Christmas with your friends from India over sardines, and about Malaysians down for the weekend to party in Singapore, stumbling out for a curry after a long night of clubbing at Zouk and an earful of Dubstar, courtesy of London's Ministry of Sound. It's about Una's, the famous Viennese schnitzel stop in Sydney, featuring the most amazing Austrian food of the antipodes in a simple unassuming lodge filled with the most gorgeous middle-aged couples, also out for a night on the town, with the sounds of the latest Indian pasha vibe from Spain's Café del Mar playing on the crappy old sound system. It's about Brits in Hong Kong who send their kids to Japanese schools to learn Chinese. This is the new culture. It is beautiful. It is also very, very fickle.

But it's not all consuming, and it is not everywhere. Twenty minutes after their last cigarette and a cup of green tea, Lillian and her friends are back in the hurly-burly of Shanghai, dodging bicycles and old guys in tattered T-shirts pushing carts full of live chickens to their timely deaths.

Yep, it's still China. Go down any back street and you'll see sights that would make the Currier Gallery van driver lose his breakfast. The animal parts hanging on hooks, the fish tanks full of dark writhing snakes and smells that rank among the world's most interesting. It is still Sydney, with backyard BBQs on the harbor with lots of red meat and a dinner conversation fixation on how many boat people are flooding in, and how to keep them out without looking insensitive. It's still America, going shopping for wicker baskets at Wal-Mart and nodding to the uniformed greeter by the automatic sliding doors with the big round In and Out stickers in the center of the glass. But that's not the only reality, and it is certainly not this culture.

Even though moments of all our lives are about any combination of those things, for these urban-minded dwellers, the new ideal is an escape to places they have been and places they will never be but know much about, to a new identity that transcends the confines of our current physical locations, and a taste of the life that is not confined by our race or dominated by national identity, but by what we like, what we want and what we are willing to pay for, no matter where it comes from or how modified it is from its origin.

In China the shift of power toward the hubs is based on the same principles that are driving the American post-Wright urban renewal. Only here, and in most of Asia, the shift is more dramatic and more urgent: it is a matter of survival and opportunity. As China opens up to a market economy, the greatest opportunities for individual advancement lie in the main cities, especially Shanghai and Beijing, the economic and political capitals. Here, the economic choices are more stark, the gulf between hub life and non-hub life exponentially greater. Wealth is being generated in massive quantities by the buildup of many types of infrastructure, products and services that are already established or more widely available in the Occidental world. In some areas, Shanghai is behind other hub cities, in other areas it is more advanced. The infrastructure being built now is set for a future that is far brighter than anything in the Old World – Europe AND America - and the people in Shanghai are gearing up for that future with an obvious gusto and excitement.

The mood in Shanghai is awe-inspiring. The city seems to change every six months, morphing into something that is more cosmopolitan, vibrant and daring than any other place in the world. The highways leading into the city glow in a soft bath of blue neon, an aesthetic touch that lends a video-game feel to the elevated motorist. Sprint across the lofty Nanpu Bridge, spanning Shanghai's Huangpu River with views to Pudong New Area, and slide into the junction between tall buildings, twirling down, down, down to the ground, and the chaos of 17 million people. Here you get a feeling of what is happening – above is the new culture, below, the old. They exist in unison and people move between the two, shifting identity as they do. Lofty and impressive, big and scary, Shanghai is beginning to bloom, and the people of the city are feeding that bloom with an invigorating energy. You can feel it in the air, on the good days when you can breathe.

The energy is generated from a two-way head rush rising from the old crashing into the new, and a new China is emerging in Shanghai that embodies this common global identity. The shopping and the brands and the materials of the new age are all there like everywhere else, but when combined with the massive-scale projects underway in the city, the effect is heightened, and the contrast between the old Shanghai and the new Shanghai becomes ever more obvious. And it is clear which one is winning: the globalized Shanghai is a new animal. Not Western but not particularly Eastern either. It simply doesn't care too much what it is or where its influences lie, it simply vacuums up the best practices and the best thoughts, ideas and whatever else that is in demand, and spits it back out in a new, evolved way. Version 2.0.

It's true in the architecture, garish and sublime; it's true in the fashion and nightlife, and it's true in the food and the service and even the way in which business is done.

At the same time, China's 1.2 billion people are changing, slowly growing richer, and witnessing this transformation and the ever-greater disparity between them and this new hub. The income gaps widen and become more obvious, the social fabric frays and rifts deepen, and the disenfranchised finally become painfully aware that they are disenfranchised, and by just how much. Like in America.

In China the growth of wealth and the ability to buy goods, such as TVs and movie tickets, the overall spread of personal long-distance communication, (whether Internet or mobile phone) and the new mobility of people who can now travel and see for themselves what is happening, create a restlessness in the nation that can only be satisfied by two reactions: to join it, or fight it. This is just beginning, and it is evident in all the other hubs to varying degrees, with consequences that set the ground for an ideological struggle between the market system - progress and globalization - and something new that has yet to find expression and cohesion, but which is fundamentally opposed to the current system. Nothing can stand for long without some opposition.

But for now, many are choosing to join it, causing the populations of places like Shanghai to swell by catastrophic amounts. Shanghai has nearly doubled in size in the last 10 years as entire populations moved to the city to look for work. Millions of new arrivals yearly, all looking for a slice of that opportunity created by the hub. There is no focus among the young and intelligent other than to be near this action. And the more successful you are in your home town or city, the more likely you are to find yourself drifting ever closer to these hubs.

The trend is most striking in China, but it is true everywhere else too. Many would argue that it has always been true, and this is true. But we are only now seeing the rise of a new global class that can move between any number of cities with ease. Sure, the best and brightest have always gravitated to the hubs, but it is only recently that the hubs of choice have gone global and become largely interchangeable – whether you are in Australia, Africa, Europe or America – only a few places are calling and they are calling equally: Shanghai, Tokyo, Hong Kong, Sydney, London, Paris, New York, Los Angeles. These are the giants. Then there are secondary hubs, places like Cape Town and Rio de Janeiro and Buenos Aires, which service a continent, or Frankfurt, Geneva, Seoul and San Francisco, which are evolving as secondary or specialized centers. Around the planet, the urban economy is driving the nation-state. In some, the urban economy is the nation – such as Dubai and Singapore – the neo-city-states.

And finally, for the hub elite, there are microhubs, the places that this elusive 10% share as their release valve, common locations with common brands and physical attributes and similar types of people and technology that enable networking and negotiation to be done in small, seemingly inconsequential places as effortlessly as in the big hubs. Aspen, Phuket, Capri, St. Barts and St. Moritz, Mykonos, Whistler and yes, the Hamptons.

It is no secret that urban places are where much of the action is, especially for the international economy. And it is painfully obvious that they are important as a market, since four out of every 10 people now live in a major metropolitan area. But these particular locations are now so connected, so intertwined, that they are giving rise to a new common identity that links them closer to each other than to their surroundings.

Within these places there is a population that is equally at home between them. It is a group of people that job hunt on a global basis with passports that bear the marks of frequent trips – of a life that is mobile, yet remarkably consistent, punctuated by departure lounges and arrivals lines, but essentially similar regardless of the city where they hang their hat (or pashmina).

This group of people lives through phone lists and e-mail databases that connect the hubs, and they maintain lives and relationships in a series of layers that incorporate the physical world with the virtual world in a symbiotic balance – with affairs and arguments, shared stories and lengthy dramas that fluctuate between live, face-to-face experiences and electronic substitutes that fill in the gaps; because their personal and family networks are so widely flung. It is a village, and a family; with an ensuing lust for more connections and a mutual responsibility to ensure that the group is looked after by others within it, no matter where they may end up.

Spanning all of this is their relationships with "out there" and with the products and services and businesses and deals that make up this brave new world. They account for a lot of economic activity, but their power is silent and disparate. In America, they are rejecting anonymity for proximity, in Europe they are seeking the variety of combined culture, and in Asia they are grabbing the life they have seen others live. Together they are all pulled by the economic force and opportunity of the hubs, and in so doing, become the market themselves.

There are a lot of Rubens and Lillians out there, and a few more people who may not think they are connected, but are closer than they think. They are the new common market, and they span the world.

chapter**two**

Branding 101: All about Odd

Any attempt to describe the new urban culture and to profile the motivations that govern it requires several basic assumptions.

One is that none of this is breaking news: I do not presume to write about anything that most of us don't already know. Our world is more connected and more interdependent than ever before and people are traveling and communicating with greater ease than at any time in history. All part of progress, I suppose. Therefore, the main goal of this analysis is to put a qualitative finger on this pulse change. The stories and trends and conclusions that follow are subjective, and there are not tons of answers about the ideal marketing mix, the ratio of ad dollars to direct mail or fancy terms that will look good in your next PowerPoint presentation, assuming you are a marketer with designs on global domination. But I will reflect in part on a myriad of stories and connections that pervade the thinking of those who, on a daily basis, make up the common conversation that is the hub to paint a picture of the new realities marketers face. In so doing, key issues will be identified, ranging from piracy to ambivalence, and the roots of those problems.

From there I will weave in some principles of what branding means to this group, demonstrating how central consumerism and consumption are to the hub identity, and the psychological impact they have on our wider search for identity and meaning in the context of the materials that surround us. Pinpointing the underlying foundations of the hub identity will hopefully help to illuminate the precepts to which marketers can tie their brands when they wish to speak to, and sell to, the hubs. Cultural anchors, if you will, to tie your branded boat.

The frenetic pace of our lives in the modern world, with so many over-lapping influences and environmental factors, means that no single factor, story, or part of this cultural foundation is truly dominant, but by painting broad strokes from many different areas, I hope to convey the feeling, the vibe, of the new aesthetic. From that, we gain a feel about where to focus marketing and branding initiatives with what are always limited resources.

These are the basics of branding from a hub point of view: a mix of basic economic principles blended with the realities of widely divergent cultural and social interactions.

Subject: **TOKYO LIFE in London – Oh Yeah Kitty!**
Date: **Fri, 4 May 09:51:23 +01 00**

Reply | Reply All | Forward | Delete | Previous | Next | Close

Canto Kitty stylin' has arrived in London? We're ready!

TOKYO LIFE Head to Selfridges which is the unlikely source of a fantastic Tokyo lifestyle makeover. Yep, Selfridges has gone all-out to epitomize Tokyo goings-on with this miniature supermarket-style shop where all of life's little necessities (such as Shigekikkusu Super Cola and Hello Kitty candy) are available. Fashion, food, art, interiors, beauty and photography are all in the mix. But the ultimate element of the experience is the transformation of a section of Selfridges' façade (on the corner of Oxford and Duke Streets) into a 24-hour convenience store.

TOKYO LIFE occupies a coveted, if sporadic, spot on London's spring retail calendar. The recurring exhibition of the latest consumer goods from Tokyo transforms a section of the store into a mini-Tokyo extravaganza for the month of May, complete with Pockys (our favorite little chocolate covered cookie sticks), and other whimsical products amid a serious attempt to export a taste of Japanese culture to a city that by May is cheerfully gearing up for the long days of summer with an open and forward-looking mood. TOKYO LIFE is more than a selling strategy for stodgy Selfridges, which last year garnered numerous awards in the advertising community for the way in which it has developed the TOKYO LIFE concept. Its use of 3-D promotional vehicles (like inflatable Japan-imation girls on flatbed trucks) is a prime example of why it has won awards, but the more clever tactic is the idea of the event itself. Selfridges has managed to develop TOKYO LIFE as a means to position its whole brand as global in nature, tuned in to the hip trends coming from the East.

This is accomplished because Selfridges turned a part of the store into a branding statement about Tokyo as a consumer universe, with execution so wacky that the association helps to boost profile for Selfridges year-round, long after the pink glitter and robot dogs have been carted away, replaced with summer T-shirts and fall flannels. Selfridges, typically associated with, for instance, old British crustiness, gains a patina of cool just by doing the "Tokyo thang" to educate average consumers about Japanese products. The sales are strong too, because there is real demand from a myriad of Londoners who have a connection to Japanese culture, regardless of their background. They may not be Japanese, but they get Japan, and want a little piece of it to help them develop their personal persona as being aware of and in tune with global trends. Very hub.

Perhaps by accident, Selfridges has hit on a major trend in marketing – culture adoption. Japan has become the exporter of choice for cool stuff, and Selfridges has figured out how to make that rub off. With Japan successfully rendered, in 2002 the theme moved to India and Bollywood, with similar results.

Culture adoption works partly because it takes the most marketable parts of local indigenous cultures and presents it to a broad base of consumers in a format that makes it easy to absorb. But for it to really click, it has to be sanctioned by the people "who get it", and that takes credibility that comes from choosing angles that will appeal to people who truly know the culture in question, from personal experience in those markets. You can't "fake" Japan in England any easier than you can fake Cool Brittania anywhere else. There are enough people now who live between these places that only the real thing will do.

[18] HUBCULTURE

<Meanwhile, back in Tokyo>

Subject: VEND OVER
Date: Fri, 11 May 15:11:03 +0100

Reply | Reply All | Forward | Delete | Previous | Next | Close

VEND OVER? Vending machines may not be synonymous with cutting-edge technology but suddenly they're showing an ability to reinvent themselves that Madonna would be proud of. Just when you thought they were "oh so last century," here comes one to make us eat our words (and no doubt some slightly stale Monster Munch). Pearl necklaces, poached eggs (while you wait), condoms that match your blood type, beetles, insurance, fresh steaks and pet shampoo are some of the products you can buy from vending machines.

OK. So you probably don't want to buy beetles from a vending machine. But let's be honest: modern consumer culture is a force driven almost purely by demand. If people want it, they'll find a way to get it; and if you figure out what they want and how to deliver it before anyone else, you can make a lot of money. Somehow, Selfridges (of all companies) seems to have figured this out.

People often want quirky. They just do. It makes them feel unique or different or special. These feelings are a good thing; a powerful motivating factor. Japan is about the quirkiest place there is, so it became a de facto exporter of cool long ago. How did Japan become so quirky and cool? A lot of it has to do with isolation. From the point of view of both language and geography, Japan is a bit more isolated than you might expect the world's second largest economy to be. With the mammoth size of its domestic economy and a rather poorly concealed disrespect for things of foreign origin, it has managed to develop a bit of a madcap reputation, with a consumer product evolutionary process that gives credence to Darwin's theories of evolution and isolation developed in remote, isolated places like the Galapagos – Hello Kitty and beetle vending machines being great examples. Who thinks this stuff up?

Japan's large domestic market, coupled with its DIY reputation, has allowed it to shun advice from others, remaining free to go its own way as a consumer culture in the modern era. Plus, Japan has huge import duties, but that's another, far more boring story.

In addition to its madcap isolationist tendencies, it is widely noted that Japanese culture is hugely organized and the society is acutely aware of advancements everywhere else. This quality of observance enables Japanese consumer culture to advance quickly, because what it hasn't thought up can easily be taken, studied and improved upon for use in its domestic market.

Over the decades this characteristic has given rise to such wonderful conveniences as the famous electronic toilets with automatic heaters and washers that ensure a warm, clean bum every time you use the toilet. In Japan there is a mainstream market for such innovations, and that ensures their success … a function of demand. Outside of Japan, these necessities are sometimes taken as oddities, and can be slow to catch on. Heated toilets may be an exception, but more often than not these Japanese innovations take the world by storm, changing the way in which the rest of the world goes about an activity. The success of Sony's Walkman remains one of the most enduring examples of this, along with the entire Japanese 1970s automotive industry, which turned out such habit changing products as the Toyota Corolla and the Nissan Z Car. All revolutionized their categories – the Walkman changed the way we consume music, and the Corolla and Z Car changed the economics of making cars by shifting perceptions about size, performance and fuel efficiency. All were originally considered oddities.

If anyone is going to embrace such oddities, the first to do it will generally be the hubs. Often they are the first to hear about these things, and being a group that is at the vanguard of consumer culture, Japan has become a consciously watched barometer for signs of new trends. In the same way that Japanese companies watch New York, London and Paris for trends, the hub scrutinizes Japan, hoping to catch a wave early, adopt it before the competition, and quickly modify it to fit smaller local cultures.

This is the opposite of our traditional view of Japan because many tend to think of Asia in general as a copycat of ideas and trends. Not totally true anymore. Part of the reason is that the Japanese economy is large enough to incubate oddities before they take the rest of the world by storm, but it is also because everyone is watching everyone, and the same group of people are keenly aware of other markets, and are responsible for the decisions about what's hot and what's not.

France, another slightly odd place, is particularly good at embracing Japanese high culture. This Franco-Japanese relationship is generally only visible during a couple of weeks in January and July, when the fashion houses debut the new season's collections at the big shows in Paris. It is then that the connecting thread between French fashion and Japanese consumer culture becomes strikingly obvious: frivolity. But we like frivolity, if only for frivolity's sake, and thank goodness we do, because if we didn't there would be no reason to buy half the stuff that we spend astronomical sums of money on, in that never-ending quest to be ahead, different, unique or whatever.

In a world where the bare necessities are mostly provided for in advanced countries, Japan's role as an arbiter of cool, its track record of exporting items that become cool, and the impact that it has on other places is worth looking at in any discussion about how to introduce or maintain a successful brand in today's world.

Hello! Surprise! Much of Japan's success is based on creativity that rises from the introduction of "oddities" to its market, led by the demands of a society that thrives on advancement and showing face – besting your neighbor with the most amazing goods. Conformist pressure within Japan also tends to squirt out innovation in other areas, creating an outlet for creativity that goes around traditional mores of society. Tamagochi.

What does all that mean for you? If you are a marketer and you have a product, let's hope it has the ability to start out as an oddity (i.e. with a point of differentiation). Branding starts and ends with the product, and if there's nothing odd about it (read unique), you don't stand much chance of having a hit. Lower price counts as an oddity, but those selling on price alone usually end up totally screwed. To digress for a moment, Dell Computer, for example, has been very successful with its just-in-time production strategy. But with that advantage it fueled a deflating price war in the computer hardware industry (partly by staking its reputation on price) and is already losing out to new lower price competitors, such as Legend. Dell has successfully figured out how to beat Legend on price with new computers targeting a sell-through point US$100 lower in China, where it was getting clobbered.

But that's just table tennis. Dell can't win the game with Legend until it innovates a product that allows it to base itself around a new oddity. Price advantage never lasts very long. What's ironic is that 20 years ago Legend was just a distributor in China, distributing, um, Dell Computers. That tends to say a lot about the future of every industry in China.

Assuming you have an oddity, if your oddity is not a paradigm-shifting innovation such as a Walkman, chances are it is a frivolity. And even if one day it becomes seen as an innovation, chances are it will still start out as a frivolity. Very few products are paradigm-shifting innovations. Therefore, the key is to make the frivolous seem necessary, and the way to do that is to convince everyone that a Hello Kitty toothbrush, as opposed to a regular toothbrush, adds more value to your life and is something you absolutely must have. The same principle can be applied through all levels of the broader consumer product universe: Manolo Blahniks are better than regular shoes, and a BMW is superior to just any old car.

The easiest way to convince people that the Hello Kitty toothbrush, the Manolos and the BMW are worth buying, and even worth paying substantially more for, is to show your audience that they are of higher quality. The higher the perceived quality, the greater the return you can command for the product relative to similar products. The second way is through scarcity – anybody can have a plain old toothbrush, but not everyone can have a Hello Kitty toothbrush, or at least not everyone can have it first.

Thus, in relation to any product, scarcity and/or quality are the two basic drivers of value enhancement in a sale, and the foundation of a successful message.

The process the companies which make these toothbrushes, shoes and cars to convince the rest of us that their product is worth buying, either by addressing quality or scarcity, is called branding. Branding is the process by which we in the modern world add value to transactions. And since the market economy is driven by creating additional value in a transaction, branding is one of the key factors that enables wealth creation in our society. As such, good branding is very important, and increasingly linked to the success or failure of our selling endeavors.

Today's post-modern culture lives and dies by branding, from an individual to a corporate level, even a national level.

Admittedly, "branding" is used in a rather loose sense here, because a definition of marketing and branding can be as long or as short as you like.

In this instance, branding and marketing are anything associated with the presentation of a product or service. As an individual, your reputation is part of your personal brand – the perception and view that others have of you, the quality of your work, your ability to execute a task. From an individual level all the way up to the corporate and national level, there is often a disconnect between the actual product and the branding perception that it enjoys.

Branding can also be termed as the conversation that takes place around anything with material value, and the process by which you engage in that conversation is marketing. Branding is the effect, marketing is the means by which the effect is achieved.

The tools we use to communicate and build our brands are only limited to our imagination: it can be word of mouth about the reliability of a contractor, advertising in the classifieds for a position, lobbying government officials for land usage rights, a price-gouging strategy for consumer electronics, anything. Some of it is controllable, some of it is not.

We can't control everything, and since often the perception of a brand by those outside is different from the perception of those inside, much of our work is spent trying to develop control over others' actions: first to convince them to notice our message, then to get them to remember it and eventually to act on it. Branding in this sense is a universal trait that is woven deeply into the fabric of our existence – like a psychological road map, pointing people to action. There may be a lot of signs pointing in different directions, but they are still signs, and from them consumers can determine which way they want to proceed in any transaction. Imagine if there were no signs – we would be paralyzed because every direction would look the same.

Critics call this consumerism and reliance on brands shallow and materialistic, but they fail to realize that this common human fascination with branding and the psychological need for people to have something to which they can identity with are primary drivers of a post-industrial economy, and thus our survival as a modern technological society. Like all things, there are positive and negative effects. It is rare, even in nature, to find a positive without a negative, so don't expect that to change – even marketing lives by vague qualitative laws of physics.

Identity and the Spiritual-Material Conflict

One good side of branding and marketing amid this drive for consumption is that it can help people identify with a group, ideal or concept that is larger than themselves, and often based on our most innate human qualities: love, friendship, acceptance, honor. This is why so many campaigns, especially those for high-value luxury goods (frivolities) appeal to these emotions.

Even shock-oriented branding campaigns that appeal to our more base senses, such as sex with underage sluts in the family recreation room, or that famous '90s classic "heroin chic," appeal to a certain, and let's admit it, admired, portion of our collective psyche. Because even though these things are not considered good, they are still a part of life, and a connection to them, if only to be repulsed and offended, validates our sense of what is within the boundaries of our culture. And the truth is, most of us are slightly prurient anyway, so a little darkness to remind us that we should walk toward the light is more titillating than anything. That titillation translates into sales, so marketers use it shamelessly.

Just as there is a common good that comes from this ever sophisticated form of presentation that drives us forward, there is a dark side that gives rise to truly unsavory things: sometimes these same feelings of belonging and one-upmanship and competition for scarce goods become negative, creating pressure to go out and blow a wad of cash at the mall when we should really be helping Feed the Children. This is true on both the individual level and the societal level. Worse than that and even more fundamental, the means by which we produce these products, and the speed in which we dispose of them, are simply wasteful and unsustainable.

It's bad enough on an ecological level, but it is apparent that we are beginning to do it to people as well, turning them into commodities that can be corralled, led and ultimately, disposed of. This is a problem, certainly from a moral basis, but from an economic one as well, if for no other reason than it will eventually come back and bite society in the ass. Why? There are diminishing returns to everything, and today's profitable consumer target is tomorrow's low-margin responsibility. And as it is generally not in anyone's best interest to take care of a low-margin responsibility, increasing numbers of people will be shunted aside, forsaken, even in industrialized, modern economies. Eventually a tipping point will be reached, and something will have to give.

Human commoditization started with mass production in the early part of the last century and has continually deepened its hold on our economic system. In the last 10 years it has become a quest not for sales but for ownership of attention in the hope of a sale. Humanity as a commodity is so ingrained that it is accepted as a part of daily life, not even questioned. But within that resigned acceptance (sometimes even enthusiasm), is a hollowness that echoes, and the more consuming it becomes, the more we know the fight for our attention is just a sophisticated ploy that has less to do with us than with what we can buy. And that causes us to search, trying to fill that empty internal space that drums so loudly.

Others are not blind to this human commoditization, and those least able to graze the fields of consumerism have been the first to scream in a wave of coming backlash, from Islamic fundamentalists to anti-globalization zealots. The suburban wives who pop Vicoden to "deal" and dope the kids on Ambien after school are responding to the same underlying feeling. Backlash has to this point been isolated, unconnected, because it is stunted by ambivalence, but expect it to grow stronger as the glossy veneer of globalized consumerism starts to wear thin among the world's working poor, which unfortunately are far greater in number than in buying power.

But backlash against what? Against "not having?" Against "materialism?" No, it's a backlash against that hollowness – a search for something larger than the linen sale at Sears. The discontent shared by those that, for whatever reason, are not feasting at the capitalist table, is the single greatest threat to the modern economic party. Regardless of the expression of dissatisfaction, it all springs from a similar well of discontentment within this supply-and-demand world. But it remains at its core a conflict between those who have and those who have-not, an age-old struggle. The haves feel empty and hollow, and the have-nots feel cheated.

For now there exists no viable alternative to our existing system framework. Anything based on a different economic system has fared even worse, mostly because we don't have an alternative to consumption as a means of driving the economy. This is because our lives are material, we have needs, resources are not ubiquitous, and there is competition for these resources. Sorry, but we are materialistic consumers. We have been since the earliest days of lore, and always will be. This has been true throughout history, and any attempts to change it have generally been social disasters. If you don't believe me, ask Lillian's parents, who practically starved during China's Great Leap Forward.

The problem is not the constant quest for satisfaction through consumption – this is all we have, since we are material ourselves. It is one of the confines of living on this Earth and unaffected by our spiritual quests for satisfaction, which are evidenced by a shadowy, unseen world of emotions and feelings and hunches. So we have spiritual/emotional needs and we have material needs. The spiritual world may be more important, but it is often subsumed by the noisy demands of life surrounding us, a material life that offers just a hazy reflection of these spiritual ideals: love and honor and truth and respect for all things. The problem, and the source of this malcontent coursing through a growing part of the subculture, is that we have not yet figured out how to reconcile these two without damaging one or the other. We cannot always progress in the material world without damaging the spiritual, and we rather know that.

Finding a positive balance to this, where the spiritual and the material complement rather than fight each other, will change how we approach consumer consumption and shift what branding is all about, because at that point branding will no longer be about tapping into and reflecting our emotions and spiritual feelings to sell something material, but about something else far more clinical and logical, based on material needs. Until such an enlightenment, the best thing we can do is recognize that our true inner selves are eternal but influenced by our material surroundings, and to acknowledge that for our material selves, branding helps link us to the spiritual feelings that we want to be connected with, and by so doing spurs us to frivolity. Whether kitten-shaped toothbrushes or Bavarian driving machines, they are our proxies.

For the hub culture, there is a strong awareness of the relationship between spiritual needs and material needs. And because the hub culture lives with branding and consumer culture as the defining point of material existence, an ultra sensitive screen has developed that filters the messages, throwing out what is irrelevant and holding tightly to what is wanted. This forcefield allows people to deflect the majority of 10,000 brand messages a day that bombard the average urban dweller. With odds like that, your message had better be tapping into whatever emotion you are trying to identify with if you expect success.

As a marketer, you will increasingly need to tap into the spiritual psyche of your customer to execute a sale, by making you or your product relevant to them. If you do, you will hold them, and they will eventually buy. If you can develop a message that appeals to that spiritual side AND embraces the selling points of an oddity, by addressing either quality or scarcity, you have a formula for loyalty.

For the hubs themselves, the development of a common theosophical viewpoint is what sets them apart from other groups within their own geographic area. Theosophical is the combination of theological and philosophical thinking – a hybrid that sums up much of the spirituality found in hub culture. It combines interest in many theologies – Buddhism, Christianity, Judaism, Islam, even Scientology and astrology (the personal guru), with a philosophy based on self, trying to connect to a higher plane from a lifestyle as well as a simply faith-based level. The hubs see all around them evidence of a need for spiritual understanding, and they seek to introduce that to their lifestyle without compromise to their day-to-day activities. True spiritual peace remains elusive however, and it is this which the hub increasingly seeks.

chapterthree
It's Expensive Being Me

Daily conversations in hub life illustrate the symbiotic nature of the material and the spiritual, and the relationship that brands play in that equation. They weave themselves lightly into our lives, so imperceptibly that we don't even notice we are doing the work for them in our conversations. Most of the work of selling is not done by a simple ad or a direct-mail piece, but by a series of light encounters that eventually add up to a conscious recognition by the targets.

The targets usually cannot identify when or why a particular brand became important to them, it just did. And when it does, it becomes a part of their life and a part of their existence that is tied to deeper feelings about their own identity, their individual experiences, and the connection between their spiritual life and their constant requirement for material items. When you get there, you have a breakthrough with person that based on the positive side of branding.

Kelly and Rob are great examples of how the hub culture operates across cities and between markets. She lives in New York City and used to work for a fashion magazine, making less money than she would like, but still living a lifestyle that embodies the characteristics of the hub, even after she got laid off. Kelly is keenly aware of global influences and her life is based around what's happening in the key hubs. She thinks she is immune to advertising and it is rare that she will admit she likes a brand for the sake of a brand. She has no aversion to advertising, but she views it as a source of entertainment or information, not a selling message. She knows that in her business and in the post-industrial economy, information is the key to affluence and wealth. Thus, an ad is not just an ad trying to sell something, it is a source of information which she can use to leverage her position in the world, whether she ever buys anything is secondary. It is just important to KNOW.

Rob is an old college friend of Kelly's who left the US for Asia, subsequently spending five years bouncing around Asia in a variety of jobs. He is motivated by work first and foremost and his consumption patterns are based on strong personal preference, with an understanding of the power of word of mouth. Word of mouth matters a lot in a culture where everyone is likely to receive the same e-mail forwards within a matter of days, from three different people on two different continents.

Most importantly, the mix between work, life, brands and their own quest for happiness is inextricably linked. Brands can bring them short-term material satisfaction, but they know life is about more than materials. In fact, they are almost anti-material, and anti-brand. But they are not anti-cool, which means they are in fact very material and brand oriented.

There is a soft angst they share that weaves its way through their consumer psyches. Nothing is ever good enough, no job, no product, no relationship ... there's not enough money, not enough time or not enough going on where they are. The only thing that seems to measure up is friendship, and even that is subject to interpretation.

Subject: Re!
Date: Fri, 27 Apr 2002 11:24:00 +0800

Reply | Reply All | Forward | Delete | Previous | Next | Close

Kelly wrote:

> **hey babe– so, i'm seeing your girl M's name everywhere these days...in every magazine! she's quite the popular one lately. snatch while you can!**
>
> **you're in europe, right?**
>
> **I got a terrible haircut on friday. i'm really upset. The color is beautiful, but instead of the funky rocker chick haircut that i had in mind, i look like betty boop. when will it grow?? k.**

Rob wrote:

haha
i'm back in singapore. europe was great we got booted
off the train at the hungarian border, then had to go to
bratislava and finally ended up in Vienna where I got
drunk playing truth or dare with a midwife. long story.
but it was cool. budapest was great and so was prague.
i've been back about 12 hrs in singapore but already
europe feels a lifetime away.

i want to move to LONDON!!!

sorry about your haircut.

saw M on MTV.uk over the weekend in London, i was like
oh my god she's wearing pink pants what a disaster.

but i still don't know if she's coming to Hong Kong next
week. will advise when I know.

Kelly wrote:

so jetsetter, sounds like you've been having a wild time
lately!
who'd you go with?? are you still dating that girl?

Rob, i have still never been to london. can you believe
it?
you have to move so i have a free place to stay when i
can scrape together a few pennies to go somewhere!!!

pink pants are bad...even on girls! uhoh..well, she must
know something we don't. i MUST see a picture. i have to
know what she looks like! anyway, i have to run. i have
so much to do today.

I'm going to dc this weekend for a bachelorette

weekend. Oh boy, my first one. am i ready for this?? should be fun– it's beautiful there right now...i'll be happy to see if my eyes aren't swollen shut from allergies!!!

truth or dare with a midwife?
hmmmm....do tell.

lve,
kelly

Rob wrote:

haha
Ok i will move to London so you have a free place to stay. No probs.
i'm in trouble at the office as they all think i've been off having a good time and not working hard in Singapore and London. silly kids!

Watch the making of jennifer lopez on mtv and you will see P2 (pink pants). That's our new name for her.

Truth or dare and midwife – just involved snogging and mojitas in a place called the Havana Club – nothing major.

no i'm not dating the girl I traveled with – we just traveled as friends – what did you do for easter. did the easter bunny come?

Kelly wrote:

hmm...yes, working hard in london and singapore.

I am so fat. if i don't lose the L.B.'s soon, i'm not going to be a very popular girl anymore. i had chips and margaritas and dinner last night after i had enough champagne at the dvf store opening last night to make me forget I was supposed to be eating only air.

But i met a new friend who told me we should date because he's only gay on fridays. hmmm...i think not.

easter included brunch with friends, and easter dinner with my friend lee, and her brother kevin that i used to date, and her roommate. it was slightly uncomfortable when lee said "it's like we're a big happy family!" and kevin said..."except there's incest involved" as he shot me a look of sheer disgust. (i dumped him) i nearly choked on my easter glass of wine! I suppose that's what i get for having dated half of new york in the past year.

so make sure you have a guest room in london, k?

MISS YOU!
xox k.

Rob wrote:

haha.
Sounds like Easter was fun. mine was okay with two friends in London and a few of their pass along friends whom I inherited for the day.
We had no such incest antics, but I can just see that image so well in my head.

Kelly wrote:

So i'm off for bachelorette festivities in dc, and i just realized I left my allergy medicine on my dresser. i am FUCKED. I will have to steal from someone or i will surely get cross-pollinated and die.
when are you visiting me. we must hang out soon. i think

we'd have a fabulous time again for the first time in ages...

Rob wrote:

k. I checked my HSBC account online today. It's negative. Why does this always happen to me. Prague last month was a bad idea.

Kelly wrote:

So i am back from dc, and it is so nice there i can't even believe it. so beautiful (the cherry blossoms were out) it's so relaxed there that at times i found myself getting so impatient with people because they're so chatty and slow, etc... i already have the unstoppable nyc 'tude after being here nearly 2 years! we decided to ditch our plane tickets and rent a car to get back because it was so nice to drive around with the windows down. we were so psyched— road trip! until it took 6 hours and by the end we'd eaten so much shit that we really should have just flown...

i was feeling relaxed until this morning when i saw this friend on the subway, and out of the blue he asked me if i still talked to this guy robert that i dated this winter. he moved to chicago, and we had this weird breakup thing...

i hadn't thought about it, but now i'm feeling depressed b/c he was telling me all about him, and what's going on in his life. all the good ones always move away from me! anyway, now i have to deal with a shoe emergency for a shoot today,
so gotta run.

Rob wrote:

> well all the good ones have to move to justify breaking up. it's not like you can get away with just dumping you like you would a normal girl!
>
> In other news i'm hoping to go to thailand this weekend and my mom !! arrives May 23. Time to move after that visit.

Kelly wrote:

> WOW!
> That's cool.
> Last night I went to the drugstore and bought products, then i went home and "self-tanned" ate half a chicken burrito and called my mom. then i found out that my dad sold some of my stocks, and is giving me the money so i can get out of debt, and pay my rent, so that is some good news.
>
> yeah!
> love, k.

Rob wrote:

> yeah. did he get over 12 dollars? isn't now a bad time to sell, what with the market so low?
>
> My brother is in San Francisco working for a tech company. Origins summer vacation is the best self tanner, even if i do smell funny. i had chicken fajitas last night.

Kelly wrote:

> i got $8000 enough to pay off my credit card debt and help me with rent.

my parents won't just give me money, so they sold some stock to make it seem legit.

i can't use origins self-tanner... more like neutrogena for me...but not religiously. i'm into the pale look these days!

work to do- gotta run.

Rob wrote:

why can't you use Origins? It's great stuff.

Kelly wrote:

i'm pobrecita!!!
i just read your website again you little snot!!! i think i can see your head from here... ahahhahaha
k..

Rob wrote:

oh that's harsh. perhaps but someday i'm sure it will evolve into a useful resource.

Kelly wrote:

harsh is my middle name babe, i thought you knew that already. who always tells you like it is? ME

That "unstoppable nyc tude" is not just a New York thing, and the champagne taste, beer budget lifestyle that Kelly and Rob live is evocative of much of the hub culture. Even though they may not sound like your dream market, the constant travel, low maintenance relationships and self flagellation over a chicken burrito is the reality for a lot of people who, for whatever reason, find themselves living in the city with too much to do. This means that they also spend lots and lots of money. Which does make them your target market. It just goes as quickly as it comes.

It is not a group motivated by the pursuit of money as much as the pursuit of an elusive satisfaction. But satisfaction takes time and money, so it ends up being a very expensive proposition living in the city and trying to keep up (not with everybody else, but with your expectations of yourself). Hence Kelly worries about every morsel passing her lips and Rob looks at his bank account, confused why it's empty every month. Could it be the six countries in 16 days travel schedule? Hmmm.

On paper, they are the exact target demo of your typical Madison Avenue or London Canary Wharf media planner: between 25-40, relatively high income, influential job and in pursuit of the latest and greatest. Donna Karan, Sony executives and German engineers all spend lots of time thinking about what people like Kelly and Rob will want next. Unfortunately the answer isn't as simple as "whatever has just come out of Japan."

Hub Tracking

Donna, Sony and the Germans search for new ideas for new products by evaluating "grassroots cool," but since they are not typically "grassroots" themselves, they often use style specialists. Predicting what the hub will want next is the job of outsourced style-trackers who pick up vibes off the street, distill them and provide them in neat little reports for a season production nine months down the road.

Take custom car decals as an example: very niche, and not exactly a forecasted growth market. But customization is one trend that a lot of car makers are looking at seriously, rising from a combination of two factors: slowing car sales that translate into more people looking for ways to differentiate a product that has to last them longer, and an urban subculture of people who radically customize the interiors and exteriors of their cars, a trend that started (in this particular form) in Asia, the Philippines to be exact. Of course inner city Los Angeles has been doing this for ages with fire flame fenders, low riders and fuzzy dice, but this is a new customization that is quirky, cute and very pop culture. Think gold, gilt and cartoon characters.

Until recently slapping cartoon frogs across the boot was never considered cool outside a small group in Asia and Europe where such customization has been more popular and more accepted as a point of differentiation.

From psychedelic fur seat covers to dashboards full of bobbing action figures, racing stripes to custom steering wheels adorned with the Virgin Mary, low-income Asia and Belgium across the board have been in love with these crazy auto fixations for quite some time. A ride in a Hong Kong or Manila taxi will demonstrate it to its full garish extent, and the practice in the Philippines of decorating jeepneys (people movers for 12-15, like taxis) is world famous for its originality and design, with bangles and signs and crazy patterns and colors that give each its special personality.

Somewhere along the line, the style-trackers picked up on this and stopped laughing at it, deciding that it had a certain kitsch cool quality, especially when combined with the retro feel of American customization from bygone days. Now they are teaming up to offer customization kits through major manufacturers to make the idea appealing to wider groups. Companies like 3M have started producing detailing packs with fender stickers, racing stripes and other assorted goodies designed to allow auto owners the ability to craft their own personal identity statement on their wheels.

For something like this to go from concept to production in companies as big as 3M and GM, they needed more than a hunch that this is a new trend that affluent hub divas will buy into, which is where the style-trackers come in. They validate in quantitative terms what is happening on the street in the hubs – from Harajuku to Causeway Bay, Soho NYC to Soho London, and in so doing divine a sense of how large the market could be for such new products.

Once it's "official," a new trend can catch on quickly, and people's perceptions can change radically. Until very recently, no self-respecting urbanite would dream of such customization, deeming it a bit tarty to say the least ... but the change in presentation of the tools that enable customization is changing that attitude. When bigger companies start picking up on it and offering such products in easy to consume units, with the appropriate marketing and public relations buzz behind it, suddenly it seems like THE thing to do. Why not put polka dots across the hood of your Honda? Especially if they are removable, as 3M promises.

The right placement and targeting of the products, talking about the trend in fashion magazines and other popular press, institutionalize it. By adopting and reinterpreting the trend they exploit it, opening up a far larger market for customization – creating new revenue streams for the companies that roll it out.

Even though this particular style of car customization is not likely to last for long, it illustrates an important point for large companies: their role in establishing particularly fringe products into the mainstream is crucial. Ideas and products can lie dormant for a long time – it is when they are picked up by companies that have the resources to manufacture and distribute these ideas that they become part of the popular dialogue. Even if they are just fads. Foreigners have been laughing at those crazy colored jeepneys in the Philippines for 20 years – but it took the style-trackers in the hubs only a few months to make equally crazy customization "cool."

The subculture grassroots ideas and the corporate adopters enjoy a convenient relationship that feeds off of itself – the grassroots ideas need larger partners and outlets to become forces in themselves, and the big brands need the grassroots products and ideas to keep themselves fresh. Part of the role of current multinational marketers is a constant search for these niche ideas, hoping to repackage them in a format that may be more bland, but which makes their own brand seem younger and fresher.

Finding grassroots cool is not that difficult, it surrounds us. What is more difficult is finding a way to make it relative to your brand and your company. For 3M, it saw a trend that was happening among car owners and then changed the parameters of the offering, by lifting ideas from Asia to a worldwide set of customers, then putting the PR machine in gear to talk about it, touting the idea as something fresh. Regardless of the fact that it is not new, it is an idea that 3M gets credited for having established in the broader consumer markets.

In 3M's case, it chose to first get this message out to the tribes that make up the urban hubs. A coordinated PR effort placed mention of the new products in regional and global style and news magazines and papers, trying to get the word out to the style watchers that something new is on the make, and that it grew from the company's observations of the street, which supposedly gives credibility to the innovation. They did not, I admit, draw a link to the Philippines, as that would not be cool. Instead it drew the link to urban cool, even though it wasn't actually considered cool by that market … yet.

This constant search and adoption distill grassroot trends into something that is a shadow of the original, bearing the hollow watermark of consumerism. Consequently, true style-setters turn their noses up at it, even if they do consume it themselves. The majority of car customization enthusiasts probably look at a company like 3M producing side decal stickers for mass use as an affront to their personal creativity. For the market 3M is trying to reach, not only is it selling the product, it is selling the idea and the creativity of the very people from whom it lifted the idea. This is almost more important than the product itself, because the only way you will convince the urban tribes that this product is cool when 10 minutes ago they were laughing at it, is to imply that it is from their own subculture, which gives it merit. It then becomes a sought-after consumable by the hub audience. It's street cred.

When it comes to who these style-trackers are, the answer can vary widely, but they fall roughly into two groups: the employees of these large companies and paid style consultants, either specialists or agencies that traditionally have been linked to advertising.

These days it is the employees who are expected to be out and on the leading edge of consumer culture, absorbing, watching and reinterpreting ideas for the company. From a career point of view, it means that being hip and groovy are often career requirements for the hub culture, a non-tangible job skill. When you don't have it, employers kind of shake their head and say … "she's just not … right," regardless of the person's qualifications.

In Hong Kong, LA, London, New York and Tokyo, these internal style-trackers frequently mix with those in their own industries and with each other, constantly sifting for the best new thing that they can take back and adapt for their own purposes. This is especially true in fashion, finance, consumer retail, media and technology, where groups jump from event to event seeing the same people, courting the same ideas and attending the same industry meetings. Over time common industry cultures have developed, and the location of the meeting, whether the Cannes Ad and Film Festivals in France, CommunicAsia in Singapore, or COMDEX in Las Vegas, becomes just another stop on a grand networking tour of the industry in which you work. It is true across the board, from the celebrity jetset all the way through to architectural engineers.

Sure there are variations from region to region, but the messages and conclusions from these shows and festivals are largely the same, and this commonality helps to keep things in sync for large, far-flung companies with outposts, alliances and competitors around the world. Events like these (whether inside or outside the company) enable leaders to communicate the new priorities, initiatives and values that local offices and assorted players are expected to espouse. This again demonstrates the downstream ripple effect of reaching and influencing the people who define hub culture, by targeting the main cities and shows where they can be found, you use them as a conduit to reach their own professional and social networks, which reach beyond the hubs themselves.

Since the group tends to travel frequently anyway, there is nothing to be gained by localizing a public message to them. Find a common identity that describes what you do or what you deliver, and stick to that message – everywhere, then use DM to follow it up with specific local product information and other details to your core target. It only confuses your target if they see wildly different messages or looks to a company because the marketing is based on nationalistic or regional concerns. At the same time, it is important to develop a clear image that does not draw too heavily on any one region or network.

Like it's fine to be French as a characteristic, but it is good to interpret that Frenchness from the new global perspective, enabling you to relate to an audience that is not French but that largely gets what it means to be French. Sephora is a great example of a French company that does this successfully. Part of LVMH, Sephora sells on the fact that it is French, but it does it from a global viewpoint. The resulting messages, whether advertising or presence at shows or even the design of its shops, are very "French" but inclusive as opposed to exclusive, allowing the target audience to feel that they can have a piece of a lifestyle or existence Sephora is selling without having to "be" French.

In the case of Sephora's international print launch campaign, this translated into a different take on fashion – away from the pouting models typically associated with the French houses – and toward icons of a globally aware consumer. From a creative point of view, this was expressed by a blonde Hindu goddess of eight arms, tipped with lacquered fingernails that represent the wide selection Sephora offers its client.

Sephora's global approach goes way beyond its ad campaign, seeping across the corporate culture. Sebastian is a former Louis Vuitton boy who moved to Sephora to handle their Paris marketing, overseeing a number of stores. Like his boss (the head of Sephora France), both built their careers in Asia, running LVMH businesses and gaining a feel for that global urban aesthetic, which they have taken back to Paris. Executives like them within the company are the expected next generation leaders, and their different viewpoint from more local types gives them an advantage that is essential for success in today's global companies. A company like LVMH is now so focused on globalizing its workers that when employees are offered opportunities in other markets, turning it down can be a real hazard to career advancement.

Nick is a great example – another LVMH executive who is on the shuffle treadmill. Sufficiently cultured and in tune with the global rules, he still wasn't sure he wanted to leave his native Melbourne for Hong Kong to work on regional visual merchandising. He simply had the feeling that the city just was not to his taste. Nick changed his mind when he discovered that turning down a Hong Kong assignment essentially meant he was limiting his career, because if he stayed in Melbourne there was little chance he would be offered anything of value again – and worse yet, he had risen as high as he could go with the company in Melbourne. He didn't realize how critical a global view is to success until he returned to Melbourne, which somehow seemed smaller upon his return. Like others who feel out of sorts in various hubs, his time in Hong Kong became rationalized as a stepping-stone to something else. The final result – he asked for a Sydney posting, not quite Hong Kong, but with more opportunity than Melbourne.

LVMH has a number of very good reasons why it encourages its employees to experience life in different hubs, but the primary reason is to season its executives and give them a truly global outlook borne not of distant impressions but of experience. This experience is a critical resource because it turns the company's employees into its test market, focus groups and free barometers of what is cool. Internal style-trackers who get the whole global thing are the single biggest resource a company has to stay on top of the trends and movements within hub culture. It's not like their title is "style-tracker" but it is definitely part of the job, no matter what part of the company they are working in.

After the employees themselves, the second group of individuals sniffing out and adapting grassroots cool are found in companies that specialize in it. They range from divisions of the big agency groups like WPP and Dentsu to small start-ups who are using the web to leverage their presence. Most of us know the stories of the big agencies and their creative services designed to allow companies to click with the consumer, which in many ways are a similar function of the way big companies now operate.

Of the small start-ups, the roles and services they provide vary but tend toward individual specialization. One such start-up is Style-Vision.com, a French-based trend-tracker that is trying (like many others) to grab a toehold in the style-tracking industry. Style-Vision operates in the fashion and retail space, selling a membership-based service to allow fashion designers and interior decorators to see what new patterns, fabrics and styles are available for coming seasons. Chronically short of staff but big on ideas, Style-Vision is very lean, but does provide a great example of the new breed of company that is providing direction to big brands.

All of the employees at Style-Vision work first and foremost on a global outlook. The idea the founders had was to create a company that can accurately forecast coming trends by aggregating material options to provide a one-stop shop for designers, wherever they may be. Working with material producers and garment cloth wholesalers, the company collects and publishes on the web libraries of patterns, styles and materials that designers can browse and select for their own use. By matching the preferences and highlighting certain styles, Style-Vision can tell where the industry is heading, allowing it to forecast trends.

The goal for Style-Vision, like many web companies, is to eventually execute a transaction between the material sellers and the designers who buy their product, but for now it is content to position itself as a style resource. The added value that it provides to designers is to organize their catalogues in such a way as to provide design themes, which make it easier to gauge where the trends are moving - is velvet wallpaper making a comeback? Yes. Where will cargo pants be in one year? Still over. The right answer to these questions is critical when you are trying to move volumes of clothes and merchandise on a calendar 24 months ahead of the real world. It is in everyone's best interest to get it right, so the industry tends to subconsciously coalesce into blocks that promote a particular style or idea, copying each other, picking up on "the trends" and in so doing, making them so ubiquitous that they become hot by their sheer momentum. Hence the khaki cargo pants look of the late '90s, and the Spanish senorita and Paris schoolboy influences that permeated high fashion over recent seasons.

Most of this stuff is planned and executed with varying degrees of success, but the style-trackers tend to be the most adept at spotting and creating these trends. Style-Vision, in particular whispered confidence, says that the next big thing is a return to dressing for occasions, an extension of the post 9.11 nostalgia for the now halcyon days of the 1950s and 1960s, when men were men, Brill Cream was not a joke, and women wore pearls for lunch and diamonds for dinner. A new sense of formality and responsibility in fashion, a return to rules and codes, are the dominant themes now, a result of many factors to be sure, but mostly just a rebellion from the casual slackness of the 1990s.

At the same time, all the way at the top, insiders at Louis Vuitton, which focuses heavily on casual, are saying exactly the same thing and will be developing upcoming lines that once again segment clothes by occasion and activity, a trend that a few years ago was all but declared dead as many brands launched ubiquitous sports-related brand extensions.

Whether in-house style-trackers like Sebastian and Nick or outsourced style-trackers like the folks at Style-Vision, the message is the same on grassroots cool: it is in the air.

By extension, the new mega trend is dressing for occasions, living for occasions and operating under a code of conduct that befits the occasion. And the fact is, the style-trackers are right – we are already seeing a new formality in business, a more reserved elegance in the evenings and a sense that responsibility is in vogue, a currency of conceit that won't put up with any slack. And just as you start to believe it, you realize even this trend is almost over, a victim of its own success, as Eileen arrives late at a dinner party and thinks, "I'm over this." She sits 5,000 miles away from Style-Visions' French offices at a Manhattan dinner party, having meekly submitted to her hostess who asks, "What is that you're wearing, and why, darling, are you late?"

The new attitude always passes, replaced by the next trend the trackers sniff out in a never-ending search for what people like Rob and Kelly will want next. The lessons for companies are simple: finding and retaining strong people are key to the successful modern brand story. The people of the organization must reflect the values of the brand, because the people are the brand. They spot the trends, they decide what will be produced and how, they identify the services that add value to their organization by their very role within an organization.

If you don't find the best people for those roles, it becomes that much harder to hit your mark. Many of these people circulate between the hubs, in a quest for satisfaction that is personal to the development of their identity, their private experience. In so doing, they are the perfect people to recruit for the development of today's vibrant companies – not only do they know the market, they are the market.

chapter**four**

Urban Intellectual Property Legends

<Friday night, any hub bar>

"Did you know that they are actually building counterfeit Volkswagens in China now? The government is trying to catch them, so they have moved the stripping and reassembly to giant ships on the Yangtze River. They plow up and down the river through different provinces to avoid getting knocked by the police and roll a few off every time they dock."

"Building Volkswagens on a boat. Can you believe it!"

Carson's eyes are wide.

"I hate fakes. Never buy them, it's just not a good look, what if someone found out? I'd die."

Elizabeth rolls her eyes.

"Look, I've only got 375 MP3s on my desktop. It sucks now that they've closed Napster. And Morpheus isn't free, you know."

David's eyes shine with a detectable moistness.

"I got this in Paris, but I think it is a fake. It costs nothing and Miu Miu doesn't even make this style, but I thought it was far better than their stuff this season anyway. An original! Hope you like it."

Natasha looks dead-on as she presents it to Stacey.

The issues of intellectual property, copyright ownership, counterfeiting and piracy are thorny in relation to branding, but of increasing importance to the modern company. There are no easy solutions for brand owners, and unfortunately, the problem is becoming so pervasive that addressing it must be a center point of any brand development strategy.

In the entertainment field, it is estimated that up to 90% of the VCDs and DVDs sold in Asia are of pirated origin. The number hovers at around

45% in the US, and 30% in Europe. Rates in all regions continue to climb as the technology behind pirating becomes more and more efficient, allowing for faster turnaround to the buying public from a widening variety of development sources.

The increasing sophistication of organized crime syndicates and rogue manufacturers, both of which are increasingly run like MNCs, complicates jurisdiction enforcement and operational tracking efforts still employed by national enforcement structures that can not cross boundaries. The gaps in the system are becoming so obvious that even small producers can exploit the inefficiencies, especially since the machinations of global commerce have become so slickly oiled. As such, it is standard for even small players to produce in one country, export to another, bank the revenues in a third and manipulate import/export quotas in yet another ... tricks that the legitimate global business community also mastered, but which required far more time and effort to develop and were previously only possible on a larger scale.

The piracy and intellectual property problem is compounded by evolving cultural attitudes toward ownership, especially online or in relation to digital goods. Peer-to-peer networking and the sharing of files, movies and music continue at a torrid pace despite the reconfiguration of Napster, which was already a global cultural landmark before it was bought by Bertelsmann AG in 2001. Despite Bertelsmann's attempts to bring the service under control, the cat was out of the bag, so to speak, and other forms of electronic file sharing continue to develop at an accelerating pace.

Even if your product is not digital, it is easier than ever to copy, produce and distribute just about anything almost as soon as it is available on the wider markets – either as true counterfeit or by knocking off the idea by reverse engineering the technology, only to release a lower-priced competitor to the market in a short time under another name.

All across Asia, incubation of pirated goods has developed to such an extent that not only is it impossible to sometimes tell apart a fake from a real item, but the fakes are so bold, even cutting edge, that sometimes the brand owners themselves wish they had thought of producing the item. This is true for things like bags, shoes, wallets and watches. Some days it seems that every brand manager has a headache and a story, making it seem like just about everything has a pirate copy somewhere, or has somehow been seconded, lifted, abducted or otherwise modified even before it is available to the public. Downright brand theft, unauthorized production, is a growing problem in all sectors and is already common for luxury goods, CDs and software. It is now moving quickly into hard manufactured goods and consumables – especially industrial components and medicines, even peanut butter.

The fact is, no consumer product is safe from piracy in the modern world for the same reason that any brand can be a producer of both surfboards and tuxedos: anyone can make anything, with a few of the right contacts.

The difficulty in relying on governments to stop piracy, coupled with the sheer competitive threat of becoming instantly obsolete require brand owners to take the protection of their intellectual property into their own hands. But how do you protect your intellectual property and convince consumers that buying the "real thing" is worth the money? It comes back to the quality and scarcity basis, in that fakes effectively reduce the scarcity of a good, hurting the owner's ability to command a price premium. Thus, producers must focus on shifting the equation to quality through service. This re-establishes scarcity, since you cannot easily replicate a service.

Companies have tried using guilt to slow piracy but that has been a laugh, especially against the rising tide of fashionable anti-brand living that gives the hub an existential reason to steal, then brag about it. So the answer is you have to figure out a way to build non-replicated value into your product offering, and the easiest way to do this is to provide service and experience. However, the addition of service to the product equation must be carefully calculated to add more value than it costs, because it does you no good to increase the costs of production greater than the additional value you can command for it.

Given a choice, many people (and increasingly many companies that buy from suppliers) will look the other way at piracy if they can derive an obvious price benefit. Since the quality of pirated or counterfeit goods is continually improving, the reasons to purchase these goods rise accordingly, a function of having to give up less quality while enjoying a lower price.

However, there is a cultural distinction behind the purchase. Outside the hubs, it is more common for people to buy the counterfeit and pretend it is the real thing, pocketing the savings while "looking good" to others. Inside the hubs, it is more common to buy the goods and brag about it NOT being real, as if a full price label or brand attachment were a sign of stupidity – why pay more just for a "label," when you can have other items that are as stylish at a lower price? At the same time, the hub consumers will also pay premium dollar for the latest style – creating a mix of 25% uber-latest, 50% authentic classic and another 25% uber-knockoff. This is insurance against being seen as totally cheap.

The same is not true when it comes to medicines or health, because of consumer expectation, a key determinant in a person's reaction to fake or pirated goods. With many items that are not necessary (those good old frivolities) there is no significant loss if the quality is not up to that of a branded good. In health, food, medicine and big-ticket items much more is at stake, and often, goods are sold without the consumer knowing it is a fake. When consumers buy a counterfeit, they expect less. When they purchase what they believe is the genuine article, only to discover it is a fake, regardless of the quality, there is a feeling of being cheated or lied to that will always leave the consumers angry, and maybe even physically hurt or damaged. The risk associated with this kind of deception is a strong lever by which brands can manipulate their value in the war against piracy.

The risk of piracy to companies magnifies with the extent that piracy infiltrates the selling proposition. It's bad enough to lose sales to fake goods, but it's a potential disaster to be held legally liable for complications rising from harm caused by a counterfeit product. A major global alcohol company learned this when they tried to stamp out the production of counterfeit whisky sold under their label. Shipped to many countries, the labeling and packaging were so good that it was difficult for anyone to tell the difference – until they tasted it. The company sniffed this deception and assumed it would be easy to find but hard to deal with. In fact, the opposite was true. After months of searching, they discovered their worst fears. The whiskey was brewed at someone's private home in a remote province in China – not a big factory, and not even a hygienic production facility. It was tough to find, but easy to stop once they did. Had anyone fallen ill, had they not taken action to stop it with the knowledge the counterfeit existed, there could have been serious legal consequences for the company.

Back on the selling front, successful brands fight for their intellectual property and trademark ownership by shifting the value proposition toward consumer expectation based on service. In turn, service becomes an essential part of the overall branding process that adds value to the product. More investment in the service part of the equation means higher quality products.

When consumers are aware they are purchasing a fake they justify the purchase on price – giving up an aspect of prestige or value (quality) of not

having the real thing in exchange for a visually identical item at a lower cost
– the only person who knows is the buyer.

Unfortunately, the hub markets are by far the worst offenders in pirated
and fake goods consumption (mostly because they have the best access to
them in the major cities, where it is easier to hide the sources of production
and distribution).

Hub culture's acceptance of fakes and piracy is symptomatic of a structural dilemma – there is little shame in saving money or milking the system
for what they can acquire, as long as they admit it freely or make a point of
it, as opposed to being accidentally discovered. Given their avant-garde
nature, one can reasonably expect the demand for pirated goods to only
grow stronger as they seep out to wider and wider audiences. Combine this
with the discounting rage that has infected the broad consumer culture in
America, and the subsequent export of that culture to Japan, Asia and Europe, and we find a recipe for an explosion in the demand for pirated goods,
coupled with a general buying preference for discounted, off-rack merchandise. The result is that retailers splinter toward either a low-end, price-driven
mass product like Calvin Klein and Philips, or a high-end service-oriented
niche product like the new Yves St. Laurent and Nakamichi. The high-end
service-oriented niche products will generally outperform in per unit prof-
itability, but they never reach the level of the discounters on overall revenue on mass. That said, it is easier for the high-end product to go mass
than for the mass product to successfully go high end.

For the hubs, both strategies can do well, but it is one-sided. For the
image leader Yves St. Laurent, the vast majority of its sales will come only
from the hubs, because it is tough to convince those outside the hubs that
the clothes and accessories are worth the premium it commands. It justifies
the premium based on experience and service – extravagant parties each
season in hub cities, sophisticated CRM initiatives that build an individual
relationship with the consumer, personalized service and maintenance on
products purchased, and more. It is so expensive to provide these services
that YSL focuses on the hubs only, knowing that its high-end status is maintained by a homing in on these markets.

On the other side, it is now nearly impossible to get anyone in the hubs
to wear Calvin Klein because it has been hanging from discount racks and
in developing world bazaars for just a little bit too long.

The realization that YSL and other European brands were on to something in the late 1990s and that the prestige of the Calvin Klein brand was in serious deterioration were behind a lot of Klein's fight with Linda Wachner and Warnaco, the manufacturer and distributor that held the licenses to produce Calvin Klein goods. Klein decided that the only way to protect the brand equity of his products was to get them out of the discount stores and to put a lid on the piracy problem – a wide ranging set of issues that were complicated by production contracts, a global network of suppliers and downward brand momentum fueled by oversaturation. Calvin Klein's attempt to protect its intellectual property and the value of the brand has not met with immediate success because it requires a complete shift in how the company thinks about the business.

Calvin Klein is too big to be hub exclusive, but by being mass it turns off the people in the hubs, who eventually influence what the mass will buy. As such, Calvin Klein is in a pickle: the company makes its money from the mass market but needs hub influentials to act as brand ambassadors. Calvin Klein is probably better off as a mass-market brand and should look at launching a new premium label that is only marginally related but targeted more to the hubs. This is similar to Armani's strategy, which has kept Giorgio Armani premium and targeted to the hubs, while hitting the mass markets with A/X Armani Exchange. All fashion brands tier their offerings – generally in three segments, but Klein's inability to develop distinction and personality in its top-range brand has resulted in a real image problem – and this is despite following a similar tier strategy as Armani, with the old New York Calvin Klein concept store still the hot flagship of the company.

The store was itself remarkable in the early 1990s, one of the first "concept" branding projects, responsible for touching-off a whole new way of looking at retail as a 3-D form of advertising. But that was then, and despite this pedigree, part of the reason the lower-end ranges of the Calvin Klein offering overshadow the top range is because the focus is still largely on the Calvin Klein product, not the Calvin Klein experience. Focus on the product is necessary, but not a great idea when the quality could be better. Why spotlight it? Where quality is in doubt, focus on the experience, which essentially builds another dimension to the quality offering.

The result? The people who make up hub culture will not pay a premium for Calvin Klein because it is more closely associated in their mind to a street stall knockoff and discount mall clearance bin than to the hub lifestyle. It's a step down for the consumers, and there is little for them to imagine with the brand. It is completely material, not spiritual.

Despite similar problems with piracy and virulent discounting for its premium brands, Pinault-Printemps-Redoute has staged a remarkable branding comeback for YSL, built on a hub-centric strategy first employed for the revival of Gucci in the early 1990s. The story of Gucci's revival has been well documented, how Tom Ford and Domenico DeSole, with the help of a new French owner, Francois Pinault, employed a new vision of retailing: to target a global universe of urban affluents with a simple step-by-step strategy: reduce and strictly control licensing, create brand statements through the development of concept stores in key locations, make the designers into stars and bring the brand live to key hub locations through extravagant customer-targeted events.

Notice how none of these steps actually involves the specific products that it sells: Pinault-Printemps-Redoute successfully shifted the value of its intellectual property away from the product, which can be easily copied or pirated, and to the experience, which cannot be replicated by anyone else. This same strategy is employed throughout the high-end universe, which is why Prada spent US$50 million to create their Soho New York flagship and why Hermés floated into the Ginza with a soft-lit building of glassy ice that was really designed to be an urban work of art.

The service strategy works better the higher the price point, especially for luxury brands who sell consumer items. But service performed in the protection of intellectual value is transforming entire industries because the intellectual property value of a service is more easily protected than the intellectual property value of a physical product. Cartoon Network, which owns Scooby Doo and the PowerPuff Girls, among other global cartoon properties, spends hundreds of thousands of dollars every year to produce live events in malls and other kid-targeted locations around Asia. Its events division is complemented by licensing, distribution and advertising arms that negotiate deals from the brand awareness generated by taking the characters live to as many locations as it can. On one level this is an example of brand extensions that many large companies pursue, but by integrating live events into the product mix, Cartoon Network integrates service into the offering they have toward one of its main stakeholders – advertisers and other companies who want to reach kids around the world.

By employing an all-cartoon, all-the-time strategy (similar to its sister network CNN, which focuses on delivering news, everywhere, 24/7) Cartoon Network extends its value proposition far beyond the cartoons themselves. In so doing, it protects the core value of its moneymakers: advertising, distribution and licensing, with revenue extensions like events that can be used as sacrificial lambs when the going gets tough. The bottom line for its events must remain profitable, but as Cartoon Network's clients demand more and more events – service-oriented experiences, if you will – it is forced to deliver in an attempt to differentiate itself from other properties that also increasingly offer similar services, like Nickelodeon. Today Cartoon Network is the #1 kids entertainment channel in the world, and this strategy is helping to keep it in that position.

The service equation protects intellectual property value in the business-to-business sector as well. IBM is a key example of a company that used to be hardware focused and is now service focused, because the intellectual property value of network consulting is easier to protect than the property value of a hard drive. By moving its business to a consulting-based model, IBM had to undertake massive changes, retraining workers to operate from a service-centric strategy as opposed to a hardware-sales strategy.

Hewlett-Packard, which has been skewered repeatedly in the press for an inability to get past making ink-jets and hardware, has been busy trying to figure out strategies to build value into their properties without moving as completely toward business-to-business consulting like its old nemesis IBM. This thinking in part led to the Compaq linkage, where the combined company is attempting to compete with IBM by doing it together.

In addition to IBM, this particular service category is fraught with competition from diverse sources ranging from McKinsey & Company to Oracle, among many others. So where IBM and HP used to be highly competitive in the production of products, they are moving toward becoming highly competitive in their quest to generate revenue from services.

Part of the new HP strategy comes from an older Compaq created program designed to harness the market value of its consumer audience with an access vehicle to other companies through the desktop. By using the computer desktop and iPAQ screen as a portal for preferred, paid partners, Compaq began a media development strategy based on icon placement. In much the same way that companies pay to advertise their products or pay for placement on search engines, ensuring that they come up first on a search, this positioned Compaq as a media owner – with access to millions in the ever evolving form of the computer.

A quiet unit of the company, the "Out of the box" division is the group responsible for building this new revenue model. By selling space for built-in icons on the desktop, it provides companies with access to new markets from a preferred position. At the same time, it is increasing the service component of the product offering available to consumers. First, it wished to partner with a media company, such as Disney or Dow Jones, to provide a direct link to their rich content from the desktop, charging on a per unit basis. This proposition turns Compaq into a media company, with necessary competency in high-end advertising sales a subsequent requirement. It opens up a new revenue stream for Compaq that was previously unavailable, and it lays the groundwork for the company to market and sell the audience to others, in the long run turning the hard box of the computer into a commodity little more valuable than the paper a magazine is printed on.

This strategy begins to turn the standard revenue model for computers on its head. Unlike the computer industry, the magazine industry is not based on revenue gained from selling the physical property of the good (whether paper or plastic), or even the content (for its inherent informational value) as much as for the vehicle it is to let others reach the people consuming that magazine to sell them an alternate good or service. Turning the computer hardware into a similar product says a lot about the value of material goods in the new age. But the reality of such a revenue flip is a long way away – the company may earn a few pennies on the unit for the placement, but it is still earning hundreds of dollars on the unit itself.

But it must be happening, because even Toyota, another producer of high-value "products," is moving in the same direction as HP-Compaq, which will eventually put the companies in competition with each other. The Japan-based car company has been a leader in the integration and application of service into the automobile, effectively turning the auto into a rolling communications unit, with the primary value of the car being split – one as transportation for the end buyer, and another as a new access point to a mass market of consumers for other companies. Concept cars like the Pod, shown at the 2001 Tokyo Motor Show and in development across the range of Toyota's brands (Lexus and Toyota Motor) increasingly reflect this philosophy of development. When Toyota integrates and sells access as part of the value offering with the cars it produces, it opens up an entirely new service-based revenue stream on the back-end business-to-business side, leveraged to other companies. At the same time it is increasing the front-end service offering it makes available to the consumer by adding content and services to the car. The net effect, whether car or computer, is the same.

The list of service applications being applied to products cuts across many industries, from entire online recipe books developed to complement Ragu pasta sauce to Vertu, Nokia's highest of the high-end phone. Vertu is perhaps the ultimate example of how service and product have become intertwined. The phone, which retails for much more than a standard communicator and goes up in price depending on how much gold, silver, platinum or diamonds you order with it, comes complete with a concierge button. Ah, the Escada of phones. But the service element is what sets it apart from clunky jewelry: should you ever have trouble getting a reservation at Kirasawa's in Tokyo, one must rest assured that the problem can be solved at the touch of a button.

Since it will undoubtedly cost more to press that button, whether in the car, with the phone, or at your desktop, these companies are adding service to the product mix, generating growth not from the sale of items, but the sale of experiences. Experiences are unique, safe from copyright fraud and knockoffs in street stalls. Experiences are safe from low-price competitors who have faster manufacturing processes and armies of workers in Bangladesh who work for pennies a year. Experiences are an endlessly renewable resource.

This doesn't mean these same companies are not in a "race to the bottom" looking for cost savings, but as they push down with one hand, they are trying hard to push up with the other, looking for value enhancement that will slow the commoditization of their product.

To be worthwhile, the realized value of the service must be greater than its cost. Service brings a product to life, but it takes time for consumer thinking to shift with the product to realize payment for additional services. A service attached to a previously "dead" product may not ever exceed or even remotely match the cost of the actual item either, but it does help differentiate products from each other. A general rule of thumb seems to be that the introduction of a service to a dead product, such as a computer, a car or a phone, should cost no more than 2-3% of the product. For this 2-3%, the intellectual property protection can be invaluable. In time it can even translate to higher protected pricing, generating value starting at 5% of the price and going up as high as you want – a tool Nokia learned that allows it to seriously consider the market for a $10,000 phone.

At the same time, it's best to avoid a quagmire of service orientation if there is no downstream value addition to price, or at least price protection. Here you end up with spiraling costs but no benefit for the effort expended. Even then, there are exceptions. If your pricing is being gouged so badly that the net loss of introducing a service to the product equation is still better than seeing your margins destroyed by the increasing presence of copycats, piracy and product commoditization in your industry, then at least some protection is better than none.

chapter**five**
Passport Please

Work, leisure and relationships are the key psychological landmarks in the new culture. All three are bisected by travel and communication. When it comes to hub living, the mix between work and lifestyle is indistinguishable, and travel is very much at the center of how people discover a global, post-national viewpoint. Growing swaths of young people no longer think by nationalistic or regional concerns, a result of early and frequent travel that altered their perception of the size of the world and the opportunities personally relevant to them.

A generation of global nomads shuttles between the main cities escaping some of the boredom that comes with stationary living. They are in search of opportunities as well as pleasure. Wherever they settle, or for however long they stay, hub living allows people to continue their experiences as part of the other cultures they have seen or experienced. It is also true that the hubs offer contacts, economic affluence and work-related opportunities that enable them to afford the travel costs between the main cities. Together this cocktail helps to synthesize the common perspective across many geographic locations.

Understanding why this new global generation bounces from continent to continent, looking for opportunity, is central to knowing how to reach and market to this group. It is tough to separate the stories of travel from professional advancement and relationships, but by starting from travel as a base we can move on to explore the relationship between these three areas of hub life, and look at why marketing strategies that appeal to travel issues work in reaching the group.

I met Scott in Krabi, a Thailand micro-hub. Krabi offers an off-the-beaten-track feel that the hub craves, as will be discussed in the leisure section later, an area relatively free of big German tourists and old American war veterans on tour with their cute blue-haired wives.

Scott lives in Boulder, Colorado and his travel experiences have influenced his views of his home country and of urban locations in Europe and Asia. Taking big chunks of time to travel, then leveraging that to change his cultural circles back home, rather than short trips with a blithe resumption of old routines, make travel a core part of his makeup. Boulder may not be very "hub", but Scott has gained his hub perspective working in and out of the major hubs, even though he is based out of the way, in Colorado.

Subject: **Hey**
Date: **Tuesday, 24 July 11:24:00 +0800**

Reply | Reply All | Forward | Delete | Previous | Next | Close

Hi Stan,
I hope everything is going great over there in Hong
Kong. You probably forgot about me, or thought that I
would never remember to write. But each day I wish I
was living over in Asia, so it is hard to forget the people I
met. I did get a little booked up lately, but I will get this
out before it really does go too far down the inbox.

My Dad used to travel a lot for work – a real lot. It was
one of the primary reasons my parents got divorced. But
one of the advantages was that he got tons of frequent
flyer miles, and took my brother and me to Europe.
I liked Europe, but it never really did anything for me. I
could not understand why anybody in the States would
want to travel around the world – there is so much to
see in this country alone.

I started working for Agilent and after a couple of years
I was gunning for a position (Business Development
Manager) but I didn't get it because of my lack of

experience. Eventually there was enough shuffle in that department, and with my enthusiasm for going after these jobs (not caring which region I got, unlike others), combined with some work I did with a large customer, I was given the BDM position for Asia and Japan.

I started traveling to Japan, Taiwan and Korea. The second I landed I fell in love. I loved the people, the food, the cultures, the challenges and benefits of being a Westerner in these countries. Being young, I did not have the respect others would have had, but I found that just the fact that I was over there gained respect from my customers. As I began to understand my customers' businesses and cultures better, I began to make some bonds with them and our own sales guys.

Every time I got back to the States, I was sad. I looked around and saw tons of really overweight people bitching and complaining. I wanted to get back on the next plane and leave.

For a long time, Korea was my favorite place. I learned to speak some Korean and read the alphabet. I loved the people, and still have some very good friends there. But then I went to Thailand. I have never met more genuinely friendly people in my entire life. The people I worked with were amazingly caring. The culture was fascinating. To this day I keep in touch with those people I met, with the occasional phone call and through regular e-mail. In fact, I became interested in one of the women I met, and promised her that I would come back in six months.

After my trip, I decided to learn the language. Really, I find nothing inspires a guy to work harder than a woman. After a few months, I got to the point where I could have conversations in Thai.

So my trip came, I traveled with the girl for five days before I decided that she had changed a lot in the time since I met her, and we went our separate ways again. C'est la vie. Then on to Samui, and then to the true love of my life, Krabi. October will be my next trip.

Some of my friends that have traveled (really traveled, not just as tourists) understand my love of Asia. Most of them don't. They think that because I am single, I just like it because I get treated well by the women. There are a lot of stereotypes about Asia, and unfortunately, some are fueled by reality. I just hate when people try to pigeonhole me into one of those roles.

But being in Colorado, there are people here who travel a lot, so I can find a lot of people to talk to and swap stories with. Usually, my stories are pretty mundane compared to the others, so it is good to know that my desire to live and work in Asia is not a strange one. Around here it is easy to find people that have been to Nepal, Tibet, China, etc., and sometimes I feel that I have not done all that much. I realize how lucky I was to find that first job traveling to Asia. I think my parents are a little nervous that I will disappear for quite some time.

I have now expanded my job search to Hong Kong, although Thailand is still my number-one choice. I am not really looking hard right now, because I am a little nervous about the economy. In fact, there is a chance (small, but I can always hope) that I might get laid off and get a pretty good severance package. If that happens, I am out of this country, and will be showing up in a location near you soon.

See ya, Scott

Federico and Aline tell their story from another perspective, with different motivations that still lead to a similar result. Originally from Argentina and Brazil, this South American couple is an example of the new Latins, a group of South Americans who have moved to hubs around the world for the experience, as opposed to asylum or immigration. The new Latins, like many Japanese and Eastern Europeans, are taking extended hub sabbaticals to gain work and life experience for a more balanced point of view than their parents' generation, who so often simply sought refuge from troubles at home. Their goal is to eventually settle back home with a competitive edge, but meanwhile they commute between two worlds as the tether of family snaps them back home periodically.

The perspective here is different from someone like Scott, who latched onto the hub ideal as a result of disenchantment with the blandness of the American experience, a growing American motivation that mirrors Ruben and Rebecca's forays. Federico and Aline's motivation is also different from Lillian's, in that they plan to return from whence they came (maybe, if they get around to it). Yet the result is the same for all of them. Despite such different backgrounds, they have the same goals – experiencing other cultures and living in a hub in an attempt to build their own private network. There is a tingly sensation that reminds them they will do better professionally if they have experienced life as far and as wide as possible.

Federico's passport outpaces even the Scandinavians, a group far more famous for bumming around the backpacker ports of call stretching from Greece to Rio for months on end while collecting unemployment back home in Denmark or Sweden, the standard coming of age for our fair-haired northern friends. Since Argentine citizens do not enjoy the same laid-back governmental approach to work and benefits that the Scandinavians do, Aline and Federico knew from the start that they would need to work their way through if they were to make it in the hubs.

Aline and Federico struck out separately but with similar goals – to see as much and experience as much as they could, with the ultimate goal of someday returning to a major hub in South America. They arrived in Geneva as students and started working. Because they were foreign, they managed to acquire a sensibility that has helped them to find a comfort zone in any urban market. From Geneva they went to Paris, then New York, and I happened to meet them lounging in Miami, where they asked me about job opportunities in Tokyo, a city they thought might be an interesting stop on their life path.

Again, like Kelly and Rob, they are not defined by money (they don't have much) as much as they are defined by their sensibility, a certain global view that slots them into a common understanding and appreciation for an aesthetic that is non-national, replaced by hunger for diversity and a focus on professional considerations above all. Travel remains an important part of their life and a foundation of their goal to live widely.

Subject: Re: Back from Argentina?
Date: Monday, 21 Jan, 11:24:00 +0800

Reply | Reply All | Forward | Delete | Previous | Next | Close

Hey Stan
how are you??? Sorry we haven't written you before.
This past week was pretty busy and it's still really
difficult to be in New York now. If things get worse here
we may go somewhere else, maybe Switzerland again.
Well, we wanted to write you what we promised before
so let's start from me (Federico). I left Buenos Aires in
January 1999.

I was studying in Argentina, and decided to continue my
studies in Switzerland. I don't really know why I chose
Switzerland. I think I just wanted to explore the world
and other cultures. My main fears of leaving home were
more related with my family, since we are very close.

After two weeks in Switzerland I met Aline, and we
started dating. School eventually finished, and we had to
choose if we would live together, and decide if we could
do our internships in the same country!! She had a very
good job offer in Thailand, and I had a very good one in
Geneva. I tried to get a job in Thailand, but couldn't find
one, so at the end Aline gave up her offer and stayed
with me in Geneva. It was a difficult decision for her,

because she gave it up for someone she just met six months ago.

Fortunately she got a job in Geneva. When we moved to Geneva, we took to living together very naturally. Geneva wasn't difficult for me, as I was starting to become as you say a global person. We had some problems with language barriers at our work, but we overcame that very quickly. Just think that our French was very basic and we both were working at the reception of a hotel!!!

Everything was going at a very fast pace. In six months, I had traveled all over Europe, was living with a woman for the first time in my life (actually Aline is my first serious relationship), had a Swiss diploma, learned two more languages (French and Portuguese), made friends from everywhere. Just think: I only turned 20 before leaving Argentina.

In Geneva, we had six great months. Our visa and contracts expired, and I went back to Argentina, and Aline back to Brazil. We had no idea what we were going to do next, but Aline came to Uruguay where I was spending the summer.

We were both doing nothing, just spending every weekend in Punta del Este. Then she went back to Brazil, and we shuffled between there and Argentina. After some months we went to Madrid, then back to Switzerland. We both knew that after that we had to start 'work' seriously, no more training.

So when we finished our Bachelor we had a specific idea of what we wanted (going to US). We went to New York for a couple of weeks to have some interviews and both got jobs here. After school Aline came to New York directly from Geneva. I went back to Argentina for a couple of weeks and then went to New York. Adaptation on the job was very easy for both since there were no language barriers, and the diversity here made us once more excited.

You ask if I would go back to South America?? Probably, but only after getting more experience outside to do something important there. I think that's the ultimate goal of many South Americans living abroad. The fact that so many good things can be done there make it an attractive place, and also the advantage over expatriates in that we know the place and we have our roots there. But you have to differentiate between the South Americans who are actually trying to find a better way of living outside South America, from people like us who have good chances to succeed there.

Where do we want to go next?? No idea. Argentina is still home of course, but for me I want to live from city to city for a while.

What keeps on moving me is all the experience as a whole, I'm glad I can say that now I would be able to live in almost any big city, and my vision of the world is more simple, every place has its advantages and disadvantages, it's just a matter of adjusting to certain things, and I know my experience and capabilities would do the rest. Every time I go to Argentina I'm more convinced that I am doing the right thing, since I know I couldn't have done and learned even half of what I did overseas if I had stayed.

I hope this is useful for you. Take care.

Federico

It's not like these two are unusual, for their story is typical of migrating people across the hubs. It's not like they have lots of money – which might seem necessary to move from city to city so frequently. Granted, spending the summer hanging out in Punta del Este, (the Ibiza of South America) doesn't come cheap, but it's really no more expensive than living in Rio de Janiero or Buenos Aires either. They lived inexpensively, as students, with all the money going toward mobility, with the belief that mobility is an investment in your life and future success – as justified and natural as higher education. This is how people experience the major moves that shape where they invariably settle, even if "settling" is for a maximum of three to five years.

As the people in hub culture fossilize into careers, the foundations set by this form of early professional travel greatly impact their world view and the way in which they spend their income. It becomes less about acquisition of material goods as it is about acquisition of experiences. The pace of life also dictates that you're only as good as your next experience, creating a need for the constant next adventure.

After they have moved from city to city in search of the right work or experiences, the group has found that short trips do fill the lust for a constant change of scene. Rarely anymore does the distance dictate the location – it is often easier for New Yorkers to pop over to Paris for the weekend than to make it to Connecticut, and Londoners will fly to Cape Town for a four-day weekend on the red-eye with barely a second thought. Much of this is due to advances in travel connections and better options in travel from major hubs, such as London, New York and Hong Kong, that allow hub denizens to take the short breaks so needed to decompress from the jackhammer stress of city life.

And everyone gets the mass travelogue e-mails from their private network, where certain places and things gain favor from word of mouth, making it all the more enticing and feasible to consider far-flung locations and cities for a short break. These are the spokes that poke from the hubs.

The following report from a hub trooper's trip to Budapest typifies this sort of grand excursion – a weekend that seems fueled by some sort of image overdrive, rich in experience and all neatly packaged into an anecdote that sells the location better than the Hungarian tourist board ever did. It's the personally branded weekend holiday experience, leveraged to position the person who went in foggy self-justification that says, "I'm doing something. I'm not wasting time. I'm getting the most out of this ... What about you?"

It is admittedly self-absorbed, but only for a moment, because people love getting the story, to live vicariously, and to know that next weekend it is their turn for show-and-tell.

Subject: Budapesti Battleaxes and Foie Gras
Date: Mon, 12 Mar 06:45:53 –0800(PST)

Reply | Reply All | Forward | Delete | Previous | Next | Close

Budapest this w/e was hilarious .... and fortunately relaxing. I stayed at this grand old white elephant of a turn of the century art nouveau hotel that houses some of the most fabulous Ottoman/Roman thermal baths and pools. The baths and pools were beautiful: Corinthian columns, marble, mosaics, statues, fountains, steam rooms, & like five different pools all with different water temperatures. Men's side, women's side. Lots of old Hungarian women, I was the youngest person in there by about 25 years. They told me in the changing rooms to go "everybody nudie–nudie." OK, so off came the robe and me and 200 fat old bearded broads bathed and steamed. What a fright. Thank God for my gym, because the sight of some of these battleaxes was enough to sell out every anti–aging product there is!

I got a Hungarian massage in there for £5 ... which was good and rough and just like a goulash, if you can imagine that. The massage room was white and clinical, unlike the opulent baths. There were hoses to hose you down and the quintuplet elephant masseuses in tight cotton shorts came out to grab you and throw you on the massage table, slap you down with oil and beat you to death. I was scared to open my eyes. Did the tight–shorts–cellulite–clinical–fat–arm–pitted quintuplet have any teeth?

I didn't eat the Hungarian goulash (it must have reminded me of the massage woman/man), I stuck to some of the more refined Hungarian dishes, which was some of the best food I've ever eaten. Some of their specialties are duck and pheasant with foie gras and plum or baked apple. You drink this famous Tokaji sweet wine with it. Tokaji is like Sauternes, and just as expensive. I ate veal with creamy tomato dill sauce and truffle mushrooms and gnocci-type dumplings, and Viennese-style pastries. All so good and so cheap. Foie gras and veal dinner with dessert and wine and coffee: £11! I need my gym, oh and some more foie gras to go, please.

Feeling like an Eastern European destination? I recommend Budapest. It comes complete with the run-down beautiful old art nouveau style Four Seasons Hotel with boarded up windows, crusted flaking paint, with only a glimpse of opulence left in some of the glimmer of gold on the outside decor. Next to it, you will enjoy a lovely cement block-style khaki green communist government building where the stark comfort will suit most (kidding). Or you can stay in the thermal bath opulence with way tacky '70s furniture and orange bathroom tiling like I did ... all for relatively nothing. You can eat and drink extremely well – Hungarian wine is surprisingly good. And the grand Viennese coffee shops are a worthwhile visit. Just the baths experience alone was worth the whole visit. You and the Austro-Hungarian empire were meant to meet!

Some of the city felt like Paris with big boulevards and same style buildings, etc. Some fabulous churches in everything from gothic to art nouveau architecture. It must have been a beautiful city in its day. I am surprised how much of it is still standing having gotten sacked in every war there ever was, from this century clear back to Attila the Hun.

Nothing to buy there. Seema's sister and husband live there, so they took us all around and showed us a good time. I skipped the disco and casino scene late Saturday night knowing it would be scary. Not sure what is worse, the Russian–styled single process bleach blonde stiletto "ladies" or the Lear–jetted–in Israeli gambling power couples decked to the nines in meringue '80s ball gowns and red power nails.

Back in London. It's sunny today and getting a wee bit warmer. Budapest was nice and spring–like, didn't even need a coat yesterday.

What did everybody else do this weekend?

Travel today is a central part of identity and of status – which is itself a function of the overarching desire to experience as much as possible, no matter how short the duration, to feel like you're not missing out on anything. Then, when you've successfully logged the experience, you pass it on so everyone else in your network can log it as well, whether it is over e-mail or at your next dinner party. Anyone who has been to Budapest gets the story and chuckles, and those who haven't will book the next weekend flight.

The concept of the short break so perfected by hub culture has changed the way the entire travel industry operates, for a number of short trips are far more profitable to the industry than a population that takes a single two-week trip twice a year. This has resulted in ever more packages and programs designed for the time-pressed visitor, the proverbial weekend warrior. In the long run, it spells the death of package travel as we know it, and the triumph of individual travel, or at least niche travel.

In Europe, discount airlines like JetBlue and Ryanair have found great success by choosing secondary airports close to resort and microhub destinations that appeal to urban sophisticates to launch direct weekend service, allowing the savvy Londoner to go from office door to Swiss ski lodge in under three hours. Alongside these airlines, new travel consultants are offering end-to-end solutions that allow these frequent travelers to hardly think about the trip, booking the right car, the perfect hotel and even lift tickets in one convenient little pack delivered to the office moments before departure.

Did someone say "package tour?" Hub travelers as a rule are loathe to the idea of anything but independent travel, as package holidays conjure up really bad mental images of transcontinental Kon Tiki roadtrips with a keg on the bus. Or slow marches past the Arc de Triomphe with about 200 Korean photographers. The new package, if we can call it that, focuses on empowerment – one price for everything you need to get away for the weekend, but with implicit freedom to go on your own the moment you set foot on the ground. It's a bit like a good private concierge. Coupled with this is a desire to avoid crummy, bland hotels in favor of villas or spas that are both exclusive and personal, often found through word of mouth or by recommendation.

Complete service has caught on quickly with the hubs and looks set to expand as more people demand door-to-door service in their short-break travel plans. Successful companies avoid the old package stereotypes by changing the vernacular about what packaged travel is, putting the focus on the individual consumer. They frame the discussion around providing services that emphasize the freedom of a personal itinerary, as opposed to hand-holding.

Going back to branding and marketing, especially for the hubs, we see a perfect example of the addition of service to the basic selling proposition, resulting in added value to the overall transaction for the service provider: they are selling more items to any given customer. Currently the companies that have been successful in convincing hub travelers to take the whole package have been boutique agents – those that offer adventure travel or niche experiences, and to a lesser extent those who take a brief and organize everything for individuals according to their own taste. For both groups the emphasis is less on saving money than on maximizing the weekend. Perhaps you pay more for the hotel and flight, but the little things that take up time, like getting tickets and stopping for directions, are taken care of by messenger delivery and an on-site driver who whisks you from the airport straight to your villa.

There aren't all that many "destinations" that the hubs consider for leisurely escapes – and much of the decision about where and when to go is influenced by individual views about locations as brands – a relatively new concept that was most strikingly articulated as part of establishment thinking in the avalanche of commentary following 9.11. In the midst of all the "Why do they hate us" commentary, Charlotte Beers, US Undersecretary of State for Public Diplomacy & Public Affairs, commented on her responsibility to brand America: "It is almost as though we have to redefine what America is. This is the most sophisticated branding assignment I've ever had." (15.10.01, Adbusters) Go brand USA! Shop NYC! etc.

Charlotte Beers may not be trying to brand an entire war and society, but less sophisticated branding assignments from the micro-hubs have been well underway for a long time in an attempt to lure travelers of all types against an increasingly competitive and jaundiced view of vacation spots. As such, we see attempts to convince and remind travelers that Aspen has more class than Vail, that Jamaica is about more than sun-drenched beaches, that Greece is the home of ancient intellectuals, and so on. The emphasis is also shifting to experiences available in these locations. Success is measured not just by tourist dollars, but by luring luxury branded resorts to set up shop, bringing their loyal clientele with them.

The Asians seem to have the edge in this development, having homegrown the Aman resorts, which sits atop the luxury hotel brand ladder with strategically placed locations in micro-hubs around the world: Amangani in Jackson Hole, Amanpuri in Phuket, Amankila in Bali, and even a new luxury residence, the Setai, in Miami Beach. The ability for locations to lure the right resorts and brands in a bid for sustainable luxury development does much to enhance their locational brand image, as much as the right locations themselves enhance brands like Aman. It's a nice ying-yang relationship. For the hub, the growth and presence of these branded landmarks make their leisure decisions easier. It is also true with retail, as these same locations seek to attract upscale retail brands to enhance their image as a fashionable destination. Put another way, would Bal Harbor be Bal Harbor without St. John by Marie Gray?

Part of the attraction of particular, word-of-mouth destinations for the hubs is knowing that they'll find a similar group of with it, groovy people – a major factor in the leisure decision. Atmosphere counts for a lot when you've only got 48 hours to detox. Certain locations engender certain expectations, and the hub groups travel with an expectation about what type of crowd they will encounter in certain locations, a savvy that comes from a combination of experience and things overheard in the static of promotion that envelops the urban space. It's a global list, all filed away in our mental BlackBerry.

This thinking is taken to extremes in the next wave of leisure marketing – the brand extension of luxury names to residential property, delivering a prepackaged lifestyle. The Setai is on the crest of a coming wave of branded residential living, where the designer name adds as much value to the property as the location in which it sits. In hotels, both Bvlgari and Versace have been beavering away on the development of new properties that "extend the brand experience" to the leisure traveler. The Versace hotel, located in the rural Gold Coast of Australia, is a lesson in luxury that the Versaces are convinced will make a mint. Marriott is convinced as well, which is why they signed a deal to develop several urban properties with Bvlgari in key hub cities like Paris and London. The thinking goes that if people like the brand, they'll love being enveloped in it – Bvlgari towels, Bvlgari rooms … all of Bvlgari's taste, refinement and sophistication neatly available in a beautiful, elegant package. Lucea diamonds are not enough for the hub. You want to live the brand, not just consume it. So they think.

Mr. Leonardo Ferragamo is the son of Salvatore Ferragamo, founder of the famous Italian fashion house. He is part of a sibling team that still runs all aspects of the Salvatore Ferragamo brand, one of the few families still running a major fashion house. The family has developed a similar hospitality extension to their brand, but in a different way from Bvlgari and Versace. Ferragamo heads a division of the company called Lugarno hotels, a company that owns the Savoy in Florence, among other properties, and is working to develop a hospitality offering that has "substance" for their clients. "The hotels have to be good for themselves, we don't use the Ferragamo name on them because we don't want to sell from Ferragamo per say, but we do want the experience our guests receive to be real, a true Ferragamo experience."

The family started their hotel project to "extend our views in terms of lifestyle, creativity, taste and hospitality to more areas of life. We see our guests leaving with a virtual shopping bag filled with memories."

His plans are ambitious. "We have something to say and to give to the hospitality industry, and we want to do that by expanding into the great cities of Italian art, and possibly European capitals, or resorts in Italy, possibly Tuscany. We want to find the occasion to create something unique and of its own personality, and for us, that is something uniquely Italian. Because we are Italian."

Yet this expression is also globalized, created with a hub denizen in mind. New projects include a series of Suites that cater to serviced apartment living, (a major trend for global executives forced into short term city-based projects) as well as a growing collection of city hotels around Italy. The Gallery d'Art Hotel caters to what Ferragamo describes as "100% global consumers", those who seek a certain aesthetic and vibe with their accommodation found in the major hub cities. "We want to bring that environment to Florence," he says.

And indeed they have. The Gallery d'Art has that "je ne sais quoi" about it that is just totally global, even if it has its own Italian touches. Nevertheless, the Thai orchids in the bathroom and cashmere throws do tend to give it away as a hub-targeted product. Once inside the room you forget if you are at One Aldwych in London or the Downtown Standard in Los Angeles, despite the creamy leather headboards and tiny balconies looking into the Italian courtyard.

Their next hotel, the Continental, will bring to Florence the hot destination vibe that has worked so well in the big hubs – a thumping lobby bar, cool design, modern minimalism and an Asian zen flair, all mixed with "the shared values of the Ferragamo family".

"We wanted to transcend fashion, to be not of the current time, but outside it, just contemporary with everything we do, from the art to the influence of Asia in that experience, by using light, music, fragrance and space all in one combined statement."

Whether branded with the luxury name like Bvlgari, or incognito under a different name from Ferragamo, both ideas are working, but not because of the brands themselves. They work because the hub feels comfortable with the other people who also consume that brand, a point that Leonardo Ferragamo pointed out repeatedly. "The right audience is critical," he repeats. And the hub people are that audience. They gain that comfort and make their consumption decisions by word of mouth from those around them, the informal group that is their chatter guide from city to city. It is clear that Ferragamo himself understands the group, and plans to reach them by targeting his product to those in the hubs, even though his actual product is located outside the hubs.

Other travel oriented items follow a similar strategy, and they know that word of mouth among hub influentials is absolutely critical, more important than advertising even. Hence, service becomes all the more central to the offering. Take Honolulu for example: Waikiki's Halekulani, is thought to be retro-stiff, Asian oriented, and slightly camp. The W, down by Diamond Head, is considered to be the party hotel. When hub troopers travel, those are the hotels that they will consider first, partly because they are on the map from a branding point of view … but more because they have heard stories from everyone about these places. They both have character, which is more than can be said for the much larger hotels that populate the beaches and often run nearly as much in room rates.

In Las Vegas, it's about staying at the Flamingo and the Bellagio, depending on your budget, but partying at the Hard Rock Hotel or at Light LV. If you are from Hong Kong, it's the Mandalay Bay, splendid in gold. In Bangkok, everyone knows that the best deal in town is the US$150 rooms at the Peninsula. You stay there on your way through town, but the Sukhothai is where you go when you are on that anniversary getaway with your spouse.

Another example of the traveling nature of word of mouth, and the power word of mouth branding has on hub perceptions of quality locations. Someone else in London tries to get people on four continents to coordinate slightly similar travels, then launches into an unwitting example of the power of word of mouth within the group – planning their honeymoon around locations that are considered "hot" by the hub. So much of what they engender by word of mouth becomes self-fulfilling, and the lesson here is the utter confidence in which people feel informed – no amount of Jamaica advertising is going to get them to change their plans for a honeymoon that can only be "perfect" if it is sanctioned by the opinions of others in hub culture – their surrounding focus group.

Subject: Paris and Capri
Date: Friday, 07 July, 06:22:00 PST

Reply | Reply All | Forward | Delete | Previous | Next | Close

Paris …
Capri is going to be too hard for everyone to get to, and the hotels are already all booked anyway. So Paris is a much better idea for everyone I think. Will, of course keep you posted. Thierry and I just got back from a week

in Phuket and Phi Phi and a week in Bali ... through Singapore. It was a fab trip, super gorgeous, Bali was better than last year, I guess that's because I was on the "romanza" version of the trip this year and that makes a huge difference. We've called the trip our engagement honeymoon, an idea we'd recommend to anyone when they get engaged! We stayed at the Begawan Giri up in Ubud, Jesus, that place is out of control. That's where Dan and Kathryn went for their honeymoon. We decided we're going to go back to the Begawan for ours too.

I think we set a date for the wedding: Sat. June 1st, in St. Jean Cap–Ferrat, France – it's between Nice and Monaco.

Went over to Dan and Kathyrn's on Monday night for a BBQ to see Lina ... Lina and her husband are moving to London from Tokyo next month so they've been here looking for flats, etc. So psyched to have them here now too. London is going to be a riot. All of Hong Kong is here.

Tell me stories!
xxx,
Doris

A friend in every port? It may sound like *Lifestyles of the Rich and Famous*, but the reality is that all of these people are fairly normal, middle-class people who simply value travel and have integrated it into their lifestyle – the hub lifestyle. Over time their travels result in a group of friends and professional contacts that are geographically diverse. The relationships are maintained electronically to fill the gaps when they can't see them personally. Schedules are managed remotely, and there is a continual watch on who will be where and when, in which case dinner or a cocktail is certainly in order should you find yourselves in the same city. God forbid we should have nothing to do.

chapter six

Electronic Friend Network (EFN)

Subject: Broadband
Date: Sunday, Nov 4 18:01:00 PST

Reply | Reply All | Forward | Delete | Previous | Next | Close

HONG KONG – South Korea has the highest penetration of broadband access at home in Asia/Pacific (excluding Japan) at 95% of total Internet users, followed by Hong Kong, where 53% of web surfers have high–speed access when surfing from home, according to Nielsen// NetRatings. Taiwan is third at 35%, followed by Singapore (24%).

Broadband surfers show significantly higher usage patterns than their narrow band counterparts. Taking full advantage of their faster connection speeds, they are viewing on average three times more ... than narrow band users and spending more than twice the amount of time online. –AD AGE INTL 10/30/01

Some facts worth noting: the average hub worker sends and receives about 100 e-mails a day. In Singapore over 1 billion instant messages were sent from mobile phones over the course of 2001, and the average user sends up to 20 instant messages per day. This connectivity is fueling an explosion in integrated living, where virtuality and reality become blurred.

It's a Saturday night, shortly before Christmas, and Hong Kong's Alibi is buzzing. The bar/restaurant caters to Hong Kong's swish crowd, and tonight is evidently a good moment, a junction of people coming into the city from New York and London for the holidays to see family, and those who have not yet left for their respective home towns for a few days of family-based R&R or to Australian, Thai or Californian beaches in search of some sun.

The DJ spins some R&B and the sounds of Shirley Bassey slide across the sleek mother-of-pearl bar, slipping through the ears of the girls in translucent Dior glasses (sipping their Mojitos and Moscow Mules) and the guys in jerseys and jeans, leaning on the bar for another round of Kahlua & tequila. Boots sway.

Just about everyone looks gorgeous, from the Hong Kong canto-pop girls to the retro baby-boomers, and the confluence of those who have just arrived bumping into those about to leave puts the atmosphere into overdrive, driving the volume high enough that you can't really hear anything. Looking around, you suddenly realize that it is one of those nights where everyone is on hand. Then it hits you that these are people whom you don't know physically as much as you know them electronically. To make this clear I have to explain the network and how important e-mail and instant messaging and the web are to the group, and how small it becomes, even though the size of the group and the distance between the people is enormous. Electronic communication is the fertilizer for seeds of travel, and random encounters in different cities add up to a collective consciousness that links everyone from story to story, city to city.

Shirley gives way to Daft Punk, the French rockers, and I turn around, bumping into Elizabeth and Tanya in mid-chat. Here is an example of the connections that drive hub culture and the EFN (electronic friend network). It was a shocker for all three of us. I did not know Elizabeth and Tanya were friends and neither of them guessed the other knew me. We each thought the other was from a separate group, an easy assumption when you consider that Tanya lives in Los Angeles and Elizabeth lives in New York and I didn't know either one was due in Hong Kong. It turned out that another person living in Beijing, Diana, was the connection between the three of us.

Diana and I met in Hong Kong on a random boat trip one day in the summer. We were invited by a mutual friend, Sandra, who was from Shanghai but lived in Germany and Monaco for 10 years working for Joop!, then moved to Hong Kong to work for a British retailer. As we drove the narrow tropical roads to Sai Kung, a northern harbor on the edge of Hong Kong, Sandra mentioned she was excited for me to meet Dominique, the son of her godparents, who was about our age and living in New York.

"Not Dominique Lee, by any chance?" I asked. Of course, it was, and Sandra laughed to hear we had been communicating over e-mail to try and meet up for several weeks. We had no idea one knew the other. I had met Dominique once or twice over the past several years through Heidi and Eileen, two New York girls. Dominique was a Hong Kong boy who studied in London and ended up in New York, but due to business commitments, finds himself spending amounts of time in Seoul, Tokyo, Shanghai and Hong Kong. We had been talking on e-mail about meeting up for weeks but I thought I had already missed him in Hong Kong.

We boarded the boat and Dominique introduced us to Diana. She had left New York to study Mandarin in Beijing six months ago and was now on her way back to Manhattan. We quickly discovered that we had many friends there in common. Some were also friends of Dominique.

As a result, Diana and I spent the fall noticing each other on group e-mails, and sharing an occasional hello and update on what was happening. She later introduced me to Tanya, her childhood friend. They went to school together in Hong Kong.

Meanwhile, Elizabeth and I had met through two Hong Kong girls; Levina and Sharon, who were working on the development of a new line of Palm Pilot covers and wallets under the name of TomTom. Elizabeth had contacts at Barney's and Bergdorf Goodman, as well as a number of buyers in the US and Europe, and had been helping Sharon and Levina with introductions to show the line for possible distribution. I think Levina had brokered the original introduction to Sharon, and one night when Elizabeth was in town on her way back from a London buying trip we met over a drink. Comme d'habitude, we also exchanged e-mail addresses.

We never got around to seeing each other again, but we e-mailed about meeting up in New York a few weeks later. Coincidentally, everyone in this scenario happened to be in New York that week, but not everyone met during that trip. Does it matter that closing the circle could have happened in New York, but ended up happening in Hong Kong? Not really. They are the same.

It wasn't until two months later that I understood the whole loop - Diana was the connection between Tanya and Elizabeth and had put them in touch, knowing they were both about to visit Hong Kong. She had attended school with Tanya in Hong Kong and later met Elizabeth at Georgetown. New York girl meets LA girl for a drink in Hong Kong, brokered by Beijing girl and London boy. Very hub.

Everybody has these stories, and the string could continue forever across a multitude of cities. There are the stories of love affairs in Korea exposed because of Hong Kong friends picking up the wrong mobile phone at dinner in New York, of people who meet the friends of friends in hotel lobbies and conferences around the world, and so on. What is important to understand is the ubiquity of the connections, and that the connections are now driven by loose networks of individuals who spread information and news like wildfire among the group. Reaching and influencing just a few people can be extremely powerful, these individuals actually hold concentrated global branding power.

What else does this story have to do with more effective marketing and our discussion on more effective branding? A few conclusions to think about:

[1] The new culture is a seamless result of ubiquitous communication and travel that spans cities, creating neighborhoods of conversation that are non-geo-specific.

[2] Most of this conversation is done through e-mail and instant messaging, which improves information and enables one-off connections or meetings to become longer-lasting relationships, however electronic.

[3] Like the networks, word travels far and wide, even below the radar screen of global media. A campaign targeted to the urban centers will undoubtedly cross borders, instantly. As a result, you can't operate on purely national and geographic concerns when you develop your messages.

[4] Since hub people are brand-savvy, they rely less and less on advertising and corporations to tell them what is good for them. In replacement, they use their personal networks to help guide them

in decisions about good products and services. Fostering adoption among the hubs first, especially for high-value consumer items and services, lays a foundation for global recognition over a much shorter space of time and at a lower cost than a broad mass media strategy.

[5] Because of this new ubiquity, reputations, whether corporate or personal, must be managed widely and with diligence. You never know who knows the people you know, making secrets and anonymity in actions, regardless of distance, practically impossible.

chapter**seven**

Evolving Communications and the Role of Corporations

One of the biggest obstacles to the development of a common global culture has always been language. Even with the growth of technology to help in translation, something always gets lost, making it difficult for any culture to fully appreciate the intricacies and nuances of other lands. The rise of English as the de facto language in the business world, coupled with a growth in bilingualism, has helped to bridge the gap among cultures, and it is true that for the hubs, English is the mother tongue, no matter which hubs in the world you find yourself.

It also helps that English readily assumes words and phrases from other languages, to the point that most new English is actually the adoption of words from other cultures. New words that also enter the lexicon are based on English, and in many cases, other languages do not bother to come up with a translation. From Thai to Norwegian, there are now English words peppered through any conversation, and eventually even the other four dominant tongues, Spanish, Japanese, French and Chinese, employ English terms for new concepts.

For the hub inhabitants, English has not usually been the birth language, but it has been taught from such an early age that it has become the language of choice. But the English of hub culture can be said to employ more international terms and references drawn from home country sources: whether it is a request for tiramisu in an Italian bakery, or Hindi yoga slang (What's up with my chakras today? Sweet savasana!), the hub language soaks up a lot of the local vibe and transports it, turning it into English along the way.

Even with the dominance of English, communication is changing due to the rapid advancements seen in telecommunications and mobile computing. The hardware and software together are giving rise to unique communication styles that will change the way we speak and write and are in many ways "post-English." Since it is becoming adopted at a roughly even rate across the world, and most quickly among the hub elite, it engenders a common understanding that does not require translation based on traditional geographic or racial undertones – creating a common understanding that is critical to the coming dominance of the new global aesthetic, assimilating into the hub culture as it is developed. At the core of the hub's new communication style is Syme, a term I've created to describe this trend. Syme is an emerging hybrid global set of communication references that returns us to the very earliest of communication forms, iconic pictographs. In the irony that comes with going full circle, we find that earth's emerging universal communication is a form of digital hieroglyphics. This symbol-based communication, a new staccato of terms, is the way that a cohesive and joined society that doesn't speak or write the same language begins to operate in cultural unison. Layered on top of Syme is the ubiquity of technology and automatic translation that can render any message pretty effectively in the recipient's mother tongue.

The foundations for Syme are found in computing and mobile telephones, where icons have become the preferred method of communication due to size and other constraints brought about by the hardware. Its ancestors are the international symbols for whatever – and it probably all goes back to universal highway road signs, but never mind.

Syme has several roots. In computers, the sheer volume of file types and programs has resulted in a similar sorting function that relies as much on a visual recognition of a file as anything else. Since most software is filtered through a set of dominant companies in this competitive space, the result is a kind of turf ownership over certain "looks." Suites of Microsoft products, such as Word, Excel and PowerPoint, all look distinctly different on the operating system, yet look similar enough that the average user can tell they are not products from, say, Adobe or AOL, and that importantly, they are a family of products.

Despite turf agendas, all these icon-based items follow a uniform role and function and the function tools within them have become largely standardized – cut, paste, crop, save, print, zoom, flip, etc. When people use these functions they are less likely to think of the "word" paste as much as connect visually with the image that causes something to be pasted. In the long run we see a disassociation with word commands and an increasing association with icon commands for the functions that we all spend most of our lives doing: creating, sorting and delivering information. It's a standard format.

The next layer in Syme language is much broader and is more related to mobile phones and personal organizers. Instead of a few dozen commands, users are creating icons to have entire conversations via text messaging. This started with the much-maligned emoticons of the 1990s but has grown to encompass a much more sophisticated use of symbols to convey emotions.

Hundreds of symbols have been adopted in Japan to symbolize a variety of everyday activities, allowing teenagers and other users to send their messages in picture strings rather than word strings. Though rudimentary, these developments are the basis of a new language form that can be universally understood regardless of the origin or location of the receiver. The fact that these iconic communication methods have grown fastest in Asia is no coincidence: Asian languages are inherently pictographic, as most of them arise from old Chinese, which builds words and phrases on the notion of line patterns that in some obtuse way reflect the visual symbol they are intended to communicate. The Chinese word for home, *jia*, vaguely resembles a house, with strokes, indicating a group of people inside a house, a logical interpretation of a family. The adoption of this communication system by the West will change the linguistic balance of power, proving an ultimate revenge in language from Asia's point of view and creating an interesting balance between the verbal language, English, and the digital language, Syme.

For the increasingly technological societies of northern Asia – Korea, Japan and China, the new icons are a logical, if different, extension of the mindset that fostered the creation of these original languages.

As the Internet becomes more ubiquitous and remote – i.e. less dependent on desktop computers – this trend should accelerate, leading to the third layer of Syme, a hybrid, shortened version of textual English which changes traditional writing into an informal shorthand. Log onto any number of chat rooms, Instant Messenger boards, or ICQ channels, and one immediately gets the drift: language is already shortened and truncated to form a menu of thoughts, feelings and commands that enable users to communicate in a way that would be difficult, if not impossible, for anyone teleported from 1990 to understand:

Syme: "U BL SCRUB OMG HES FFC DING"
English: "You hooked up with that guy?! You are such a ho! Oh my God he is really cute, call me and tell me more."

As communication becomes more and more common on a numeric and symbolic keyboard, with a menu of digital icons that convey standard associations, we find ourselves operating in a new world of language that is not based on the old conventions of nationality, geography and race. It is instead based on communication standards hosted through corporations, the entities that control access to the software, content and communication platforms. Companies like Nokia, AOL Time Warner, Viacom and NTT DoCoMo in turn have little power to manipulate the new standards or the look of Syme as it develops, because it arises as an organic function of users themselves, who, in the absence of a standard and the need to communicate RIGHT NOW, will invariably think of a way to say what they want with no regard to old convention.

Changes in language and communication have always crept up from the masses – how many times have we heard that Webster's Dictionary has added a new word to the "official" lexicon – but the Internet and mobile revolution has put the changes on speed, while removing obstacles to distribution. The net effect – if it's a good idea, if it's easier to read and understand, and if it makes communication faster, an innovation in Syme can be adopted at lightning speed, globally.

Youths invariably have the edge in this game, as they do in many aspects of the information revolution. Even with the collapse of the Internet bubble and subsequent routing of various dotcom poster-children, the inherent competitive advantage of youth is obvious. The youthful ability to shed existing mores for new ones without much psychological loss means that innovations in the Syme department will likely be led by teenage girls in Osaka trying to figure out how to text message the Matsuzakaya sales girl. "Hold the pink stilettos in a size 4," rings eternal while in another window they hold a simultaneous voice conversation with the muy guapo > > > > (Net hookup) they met the other day on the corner after a Net rendezvous. At the same time they will also be fumbling for the electronic key code for entry onto the subway. Time is of the essence, and we don't have time to say what we mean, let alone type it. Let's multitask. Therefore we abbreviate.

Because Syme is built on the backbone of our current communication systems like e-mail, instant messaging, and multimedia messaging, everyone is enjoying significant input to its development, erasing the old arguments about cultural hegemony. It's very democratic, because it operates by the rules of our old friends supply and demand - an endless supply of new strings, terms and icons is created regularly, and the demand for them, based on their relevance and usefulness as opposed to their origin, cements their survival.

For instance, the online Chinese community has been busy creating a numeric-based language that is about three steps removed from Chinese, yet once explained becomes easily adopted by other, non-Chinese speaking users. To think that the human mind is beginning to understand and think in numeric code is most interesting indeed. Perhaps it is the first step to eventually thinking binary – in the code of computers themselves. In some Asian cultures it is common to associate certain numbers with unrelated terms because orally, they sound similar. For instance, the number for four in Chinese sounds like the word for death, and is thus considered unlucky. Online, the number four has thus become a proxy for negativity and unpleasantness. Similarly the number eight sounds like rich, or wealth. This number is thus associated with positive and pleasant concepts, or even just with wealth. The number two is associated with "more," so "24" can mean very bad and "224" can mean horrible, just like "28" can mean "really rich."

Chinese speakers have developed entire numeric strings based on this thinking, such that a sequence of numbers can be interpreted as an entire statement. Combine this with truncated English and the ever-expanding selection of icons, and our shorthand becomes the new base of our common electronic language.

Which brings us to another interesting point – hub culture enjoys a peculiar anomaly that could hardly have been predicted before the popular rise of the Internet and text messaging: we have become so adept at communicating through e-mail and text-based communication (even this rudimentary Syme), that we are beginning to forget how to write with pen and paper. Ask urban professionals in any hub the last time they picked up a pen and wrote something of any length, and if they are under 30, chances are they have grown unaccustomed to handwriting much beyond meeting notes in a scrawl. If they do write much, it is probably peppered with the new handwriting standard of icons and letter and number strings that are the hybrid language of the mobile generation. Encouraged by the computer, the BlackBerry and the Palm, we have even standardized the process in which we write individual alphabetical letters.

The Communications Powerplay

A visit to NTT DoCoMo's head office in Tokyo highlights the future feel of this brave new world of communication. In meetings with company executives and Keiji Tachikawa, President and CEO, it is clear that Japan is consolidating a leadership position in next generation communications. Fortunately Ericsson, the Swedish giant, has realized this, and subsequently scrapped its consumer handset business in favor of an alliance with Sony. This smart move allows Ericsson to focus on expanding their core horizontal businesses while allowing a better-suited partner to move vertically for the company. (There is more on this type of marketing strategy in Chapter 14).

As Japan vies for control of the industry's further development, top executives at other Japanese companies, such as Toshiba, NEC and Mitsubishi, say the key to Japanese dominance will no longer be hardware, but software. NTT DoCoMo is a software company, first and foremost, and it thinks like a software company. In demonstrations of its products, top executives repeat this point, and stress the fact that despite the company's hiccups with service and reliability (NTT DoCoMo recalled several recent models, and the launch of third generation (3G) was delayed to October 2001, with only limited availability around Tokyo), it is still the first to market with broadband appliances, and this first-mover advantage is invaluable in the software communications war.

In Japan alone, DoCoMo is already very concerned about rising competitors in the race to own 3G, namely Vodaphone, associated with France Telecom and increasingly powerful in the global telecom field, as well as KDDI, a Japanese based national player that tends to copy and produce similar technology at a lower cost. DoCoMo's answer is to try and innovate as quickly as possible while building a brand name now for markets it won't enter for at least one or two years. Rollout in South Korea and Hong Kong is not expected until at least 2003, but the company is already very active in its communications strategy across these and other Asian markets.

NTT DoCoMo's stake in AT&T Wireless is also not expected to bear fruit on the consumer sales side until even later than 2003. Despite the lag, the company is taking steps now to lay the groundwork for market entry into the US. A coordinated press and branding campaign has been underway since 1999, laying the visibility frameworks in the US and other future key markets even when the company has nothing yet to sell. This has been matched by equity investments in potential future rivals NTT Docomo is turning into partners, such as AT&T Wireless and Hutchison in Hong Kong.

You get a good feel of what the DoCoMo future is like talking to senior executives like Tachikawa-san. His perspective is direct and his mission is clear: NTT DoCoMo is about "service, service, service, and changeable service." The key here is not the service, but that it is changeable, and changeable service is about software. Strong software is the primary device that enables the company to change, expand and tailor the features of its offering. Remember, this company makes money on every service the user downloads, collecting a few yen for every bit of data that a customer punches up. As such, hardware is not the key because usage of services becomes the profit stream, whether it is AOL integrated chat bundling or downloading CNN headlines.

Japan has a continuity that does not exist in the West, and a Zen aesthetic that is unique to its culture. The nice thing about NTT DoCoMo, and perhaps the key to the company's success, is that it has taken that Zen aesthetic, commonly associated with form, function and minimalism in the West, and taken it back to older Japanese roots, the ideas that form and function are not disparate and that "Zen" is simply the systemic and organized order of materials. Not necessarily less materials (or services), as seen in traditional Western Zen minimalism, just organized. NTT DoCoMo phones eschew frills and embrace functionality in a way that makes them truly Japanese and Zen-like in the traditional form, while embracing multifunctionality at the same time. The key is in the expression.

Mari Matsunaga, who is widely credited with developing the architecture of the I-mode, which in turn was the basis for the new 3G models, has been quoted as saying that the idea behind the development of this software was a convenience-store model: to try and put the items that a customer needs in as close proximity and with greatest ease of use as possible to the user. She actually studied the floor plan of convenience stores and thought about a similar layout of services in the phone system architecture.

In addition to the development and layout of the services, DoCoMo has taken this thinking vertical. DoCoMo's version of 3G works on a standard called UMTS, or the Universal Mobile Telephone System, a standardized format that allows functionality across all devices introduced to the market. It is a little bit like the Sony Memory Stick strategy, linking a suite of products together, offering users the ability to buy a whole range of items that can work and fit seamlessly. It's called integration and Korean companies like LG and Samsung are very busy right now figuring out how to similarly link all your home appliances.

The series of 3G phones illustrates the point perfectly. Based on FOMA (short for the quirkily cute Freedom of Multimedia Access), the concept is supremely simple: ubiquitous connection on all devices. Thus, whether you are using a videophone, a wireless Internet port, an Eggy (multimedia walkman), or just a standard e-mail/phone device, the architecture is all based on the same system and linked to the same NTT Communications network. The devices are truly next generation: the video-phone (P210 series) allows users to see one another as they talk, causing chagrin from women everywhere as they reach for lipstick when the phone rings, and men who are found suddenly patting flyaway hair before they go "onboard."

DoCoMo sold out its entire stock of 9,000 3G models in the first three weeks after launch – a combination of the video-phone, a standard 3G heavy-duty phone that downloads JAVA applets and features a super-bright screen that eliminates glare and allows people to play advanced video games on their way between meetings (or in them). There is even a cool wireless Internet card that plugs directly into a standard PC. Flip the antennae up on the Internet card and you're up and running with a wireless connection, able to download movie clips and web content at lightning speed. It rocks.

The ubiquitous platform and the fun functions of the DoCoMo advances have infected the entire company, and to some extent the country itself. DoCoMo has created a phenom with 38 million subscribers, 28 million of which are on the old I-mode service, which is already leaps and bounds ahead of anything on offer in the US and Europe. Sales of the new 3G system are expected to top 150,000 the first six months after the launch of the new FOMA service, and with DoCoMo claiming 99.7% coverage in the Tokyo area, it is likely that consumers will not only top their initial expectations but continue to match supply with over-demand for the near future.

DoCoMo becomes interesting from a marketing point of view when you consider how successfully it has integrated the philosophy of its products with every aspect of the customer experience; and how that translates into the company's larger business-to-business activities.

Step through the double doors of the shiny new NTT DoCoMo building in downtown Tokyo, and you begin a journey. Pass some guards and step into giant marble-floored express elevators, easily triple the size of a normal elevator, giving you the impression of space, and freedom. It glides silently to the 27th floor, where the doors slide open with a whoosh, depositing you squarely five years into the future. On either side, bright sunlight spills onto the highly polished floors of a sleek, cavernous, yet surprisingly warm hall, faced on either side by grand windows with sweeping views of Metropolitan Tokyo: 18 million mobile consumers in every direction, tipping over the horizon into an unimaginable distance.

The office hums. People flit to and fro, and as you get your bearings, the eyes are drawn to the complicated DoCoMo logo, and the words *Do Communications over the Mobile Network*.

Hmmm. That makes sense.

Below the lighted sign and with their backs to the masses of Tokyo, are eight women of immaculate perfection, tending phones and visitors in three sweeping arcs of reception banks, all matching in pink twill, all perfectly polite and absolutely frightening in their picture of some well imagined, Star-trekkian future. Low seats with no backs wait on either side of the immense lobby, and visitors mill around looking at the Japanese parliament building, squat and staid below.

All together, it is a corporate version of T8, the restaurant Lillian visited with her friends in Shanghai. The design is minimal in the Philippe Starck sense, and the low murmur of languages drifts from those executives milling around in wafts of German and Chinese and Japanese and English. The feeling is that you have stepped into a world where nationalism is just another part of the décor, as interchangeable as the rugs or the paintings on the wall. It feels post-industrial, and strangely post-capitalist. Maybe it is just a sophisticated front for a very profitable organization, or maybe it is a next-generation corporation that derives value from the trading of communication. Either way, every part of the company reflects the ideals of hub culture.

And it is ideal for the hub, because the products DoCoMo sells are designed to mesh so many disparate products surrounding our consumption of information into one unit. Everything about DoCoMo is related to creating an egalitarian world of ubiquity in communication. It is reflected in the corporate culture and is therefore expressed in the physical surroundings it has created. It feels like non-egoist capitalism, the opposite of the Randian worldview, the industrial view of capitalism. If I'm right, it is a precursor of a new relationship between companies, products and people, a new egalitarianism that comes with flat hierarchies open to information access. It feels like these ideals could easily go a step further, embracing a spiritual sense of superiority by virtue of the service it performs as a company, something that the company's customers can relate to and identify with that go beyond simple consumption. Or it could just be another company with cool products and a nice lobby.

chaptereight
Relationships

Eileen: "Even if I found what I am looking for, I don't have time for it."

Hub Love

Creeping forward like some sort of glacial floe, the overriding preoccupation with age and relationships seems to have avoided much of hub culture's external psyche. With so much going on, age tends to fall by the wayside until one day when you wake up and notice that the glacier has crept into your backyard, and it's just you and the Botox bills. But until that day, at some point in your early 40s for a woman, and for a guy, the late 40s, everything seems to just coast along. You are surrounded by troopers at your side searching for "the one," and everyone stops for a five-day mourning at a tropical resort when one goes down, but mostly, things just keep rolling in the blur that is hub life.

Nevertheless, since the relationship is a central facet of discussion and identity for the hub, here are a few types of hub relationships that outline where most hub people fall. These will be great for the next time you are trying to think up consumer categories for your product-positioning meeting.

[1] BiMs – Bicultural Marrieds. The expression of an ultimate hub relationship in which not only do you experience as much diversity as possible through travel and communication, you make it a permanent part of your life. Many hub troopers do not want to marry someone from their own background, because that's, well, boring. By choosing someone from somewhere else – as culturally diverse as possible – they cement an acceptance of diversity

into their life. Biracial couples in this group enjoy the added satisfaction that comes with knowing they will have the best-looking kids and often, multiple passports.

[2] LTM – Long-Term Monogamous. A large portion of hub culture fits into this group. In a serious relationship but unwilling to tie the knot for fear of "losing the magic." Living together but largely independent and career focused. Financially separate. Haven't quite figured out the kids thing.

[3] SLDR – Serial Long-Distance Relationship. Nobody at home is good enough, and the only interesting people tend to be found at dinner parties in far away cities. Allows the trooper to focus on handling daily life without the added pressure of fighting over who picks up the dry cleaning. Facilitates expensive but comfortably regular drunk dialing.

[4] S "NW" – Single, "Not Worried." Have the kids thing figured out, because by the time they want them they can:
[a] Bioengineer;
[b] Do a next best thing … "I have a friend. It will work with us;"
[c] Adopt from Lithuania. This group of people says they are too busy with career and living to worry about relationships. Totally worried.

Please note that none of these categories is gender specific, which is itself a statement about hub culture's attitude toward many aspects of equality and diversity.

BiMs

Markus and Anna met about three years ago in Hong Kong. He was a lawyer from New Zealand, working for a large firm and trying to get ahead so that he could do what everybody in the hubs works to do: afford to leave. She was a trainee, fresh off the boat from Boston on an internship. They were introduced through a German guy who worked at her firm, a friend of Markus. Very typical of the new paradigm.

Anna is one of the loudest girls you could meet and totally blows away conventional stereotypes about the quiet, intelligent Asian elite. Though her parents are from China, she was born and raised in America. Like many American-born Chinese (ABC), she always had an interest in Asia (and China in particular) but never really expected to end up back in the region. Yet like the New Latins, many Asian Americans now see benefits of their biculturality and come back with international perspectives. Once back, they realize that the Asia they grew up hearing about is not the Asia that exists today. As Tara, a similar Chinese-Canadian says,

"We have a romanticized view of China. We believe that everyone in Asia is full of filial love and family respect, because that's the way it was when our parents left. Then you get here and you realize it's not filial at all. They treat old people as badly as we do, only at least we feel guilty about it. Have you ever seen an 80-year-old woman pushing a cart of cardboard recycling up a hill in Vancouver? I don't think so."

I digress. For Chinese especially, the long term seems to have always existed in Mother China, not America. Like many Americans who studied at good schools during the '90s, upon graduation Anna found that greater opportunities existed outside the US than in secondary cities such as Boston. So she applied for an internship and rocked up one summer, armed with a few e-mail addresses of friends of friends scattered around the region.

Anna is the kind of girl who opens her mouth and spits out whatever electronic impulse has just crossed the front of her head. The voice, high pitched and sharp, provides an effective weapon in the inevitable verbal spars that develop in any conversation to which she is privy. Intelligent, beautiful, quick-witted and disarmingly funny, she always wins. Markus learned very early on that if he was to have any success with a woman of this caliber, he would have to bend like a willow, grin and simply nod his head. The rest of his friends, used to a more demure type of female, quickly realized they had a live wire on their hands and duly kept their distance.

Out sailing on the weekends, Markus would inevitably take the jabs about his new girlfriend, with the typical guy conversation revolving around whether or not she was as loud behind closed doors as she was sitting at the Dublin Jack, sipping a pint of Stella. Markus inevitably cut the comments off with a knowing smile and an agile disappearance down the hatch in search of a bucket of Heineken, avoiding the answer with a sly grin on his face. A certain envy persisted among the group – Markus had found someone who fulfilled every inch the antithesis of the Suzie Wong stereotype: sophisticated, confident, independent, and proud to be who she was.

There is a lingering Suzie Wong perception when people think of mixed couples, especially within Asia. The stereotype of Western men out hunting at fertile hotel bars packed with Singapore party girls does remain true to some extent, but Markus and Anna became a great example of the hub's disdain for these old cliches.

Here, Anna was the catch, not Markus (as great a guy as he is). Together they made a great team with a relationship based on respect. They soon settled into the lifestyle of a SLDR couple. When she went back to Boston to finish school, Markus would commute to New York every couple of months to meet up. It's generally easy to justify business in one of the big hubs – even without a specific agenda, since most large companies have offices in the major cities.

So she would drive down from Boston and he would fly in from Hong Kong, and New York became the base. When time permitted, they would meet in other locations. A winter ski trip at Whistler (halfway point between Asia and North America), or a long weekend in London, the other halfway point, would generally fill the gaps between longer visits.

When she finished school, Anna used the contacts she had made during the previous summer to land a practicing slot at another of the big firms, starting a circuit of professional flotation that will probably last her whole career.

Professional flotation is the best term to describe the tendency for today's global professional classes to float among a fixed number of market players in any particular industry. Consulting, media, banking, law and retail all operate within fixed, overlapping circles across hubs, and players tend to bounce between a limited world of five to seven competitors once their sights are fixed on a particular discipline.

Over time Anna's and Markus's existence became more intertwined, until the point where it was no surprise when they announced their engagement over e-mail to friends in about nine different countries, fixing the date for late spring and ensuring that Anna would have her day as a May bride.

Weddings are not easy, especially for a BiM couple like Anna and Markus. With his family in Australia, New Zealand and the UK, and her family in China, Boston and New York, the logistics alone require a determination that rivals the coordination of a small economic conference. Many such couples tend to choose the five-day party route, in which villas in Bali or Phuket or St. Kitts and Nevis are rented and various friends and family are forced into an involuntary mini-vacation filled with Mai-Tais and twilight visits to sample local culture. M&A decided to confine that scenario to their respective stag parties and opted to marry in Hong Kong, their temporary home.

Out went the e-mail, complete with a PowerPoint show featuring Markus on bended knee somewhere in Mauritius proposing to his bride to be. Then came the invites, in a mix of Chinese and Western script, with carefully planned equal emphasis on the both. From a cultural point of view, both couples would be considered Western, but a sense of tradition endures, and the result was a balanced, bicultural affair.

In traditional Western ceremonies, the emphasis of the event is usually on the church service and ceremony that bind the couple together, followed by a dinner reception and party. In Chinese ceremonies, an elaborate network of familial visits the morning of the wedding is followed by a large banquet the evening of the event. The family visits are exceptionally important, and this is where the focus of the day rests.

The guests themselves focus on the part of the ceremony they have the most experience with, but quickly get used to the customs that encompass the ceremony. As such, there are not many people who don't know firsthand about the Indian rites, the French custom, or the Latin dances that make reception banquets different, and so similar.

Lather, rinse, repeat. Over the course of the last year, I can think of several other bicultural couples who have gone through similar scenarios – with the only difference being the location. Maybe it's the Indian wedding in Singapore, the Chinese gala in San Francisco, or the French guy who eloped to Tokyo with his Australian girlfriend (so French). All of them wanted a relationship that matched their lifestyle, with a person who connected to the same ideals that were important to them. Together, they make it work across old boundaries, and in so doing, become the new norm.

When it comes to kids with this group, there appears to be a transfer of materialism away from the parents and onto the kids. The quest for experience becomes less about the parents trying to get everything in, and more about them getting the kids into everything. This translates into fencing lessons and language tutors and aptitude tests and uber-camp, skill set courses to assist in hyper-emotive personal development. Certainly this is driven by love and the traditional desire for parents to see their kids do well, but is still reflective of the quest for experience that permeates the hub. It's all Baby Dior and having the right nanny, regardless of the cost, to make sure the kids grow up with the right "influences and perspectives."

At the same time they pat themselves on the back, proud that they are "over the scene" of being single or pleased that they have finally "grown up", there is an inevitable halt and red-faced giggle when they realize they have just moved the goal posts from them to the kids in terms of the hub's consumption perspective.

LTM

Nick and Rachel are evocative of the LTM relationship – the kind that is far more common than the utopian ideal "let's get married" but not quite Sex in the City either. This South African and German rely on each other and live their life together, but neither is willing to become "dependent" on the other. They spend a lot of time telling their friends how frustrating the relationship is, but they find solace in each other and in many ways are a perfect fit, because they give each other enough space and respect in the relationship to do their own thing. By and large, when one needs the other, he or she delivers.

But don't expect Nick and Rachel to get married. The financial and social trappings that come with marriage don't overtly appeal to them, and because they are part of a generation that has seen divorce first-hand, they are far more hesitant to tie the knot until it can deliver some sort of perfect life. They both know it never will. Because their relationship has lasted longer than some marriages, they derive a certain sense of security from their lack of formal commitment, their respect for the other's freedom. This is not meant to imply both are out sleeping around, for the lack of structure has had an opposite effect. But if one got transferred to Tokyo tomorrow, chances are both of them would not go.

They also keep their financial matters separate. During the dot-com era, when Rachel was doing well on telecom stock options, she used those profits to build security for herself. Later, when the global markets started their downward spiral and she lost her cushion, she sold her half of their flat to Nick, because the mortgage payments were too high for her, and Nick charged her rent. Would that happen if you were married? Not likely. Would that happen in a culture where even love is a second priority to the grand plan and desire for freedom and self-sufficiency? Yep.

The two have reached a plateau in the relationship and are not likely to see a change unless there is an external shock, after which they will either go their separate ways in search of another LTM, or quickly plunge into the world of BiMs.

Fridge Magnets (divorced but friends, with all the snapshots of your ex still on the fridge) also share similar characteristics. These are people who got married, possibly had a child or two, then divorced. With no kids, they settle into a friendship that allows them to stay in touch and observe the various foibles of their former partner with a quiet smirk, "because really, what's marriage but just a deeper relationship …"

For those with kids, being friends seems like the responsible thing to do, and not as hard as it was for our parents. Perhaps it's because hub culture automatically assumes nothing is really permanent. It could also be that people hate admitting mistakes, and feel like if they loved them once, they can't be all that bad just because they got divorced. But more than that, it is about practicality. Provided both parents are reasonably hub, and thus consumed with their brand of socially responsible integrity, they subsequently realize that raising kids is actually much easier on their life when they can offload them on a regular basis … three days here and four days there. The Christian Coalition would object to that as a conscious lifestyle choice, but it doesn't seem to be too bad for the kids – they get to see both parents, and the parents get a break from the kids that allows them to feel like they are not missing out on anything by being a parent; which makes them a better parent during the time that they are together. Parenting for many, these days, is such a double-edged sword. It is so expensive, but so fundamental. Arrangements like this help LTMs and Fridge Magnets juggle more, more easily. The downside is that kids sometimes become the managers of their parents.

SLDR

The long-distance relationship is the love crutch of hub culture, that special girl or boy in another port who stops you from thinking you are sacrificing love for lifestyle. It also fits nicely with the lifestyle, providing a solid excuse to travel at the drop of a hat, because that relationship is "so" important, and if you don't spend the weekend together in Aspen, how are you ever going to figure out if this is "the one?" There should be special LDR airfares, complete with condoms and roses at check-in.

It is an alluring illusion for the perpetually busy. The day-to-day work that it takes to manage a close relationship, a luxury that tends to hit the back burner in the demands of day-to-day life, can be replaced with the "idea" of a relationship, which is often more effective in managing emotional stress than an actual relationship. It also fits well with the proximity and image management issue we discuss elsewhere. It's so much more convenient to tell your friends about a hot weekend in Bangkok than to drag your stumplehead partner to cocktails so she can complain about how she just wants to be somewhere else.

Claire: "How often have you wanted to go to Taichung? It's at the ass end of nowhere. And how do I justify business dinner expenses that include three bottles of Moet? That got a bit out of hand. At least I got to go back to the office with a big grin on my face, so everyone could ask me why I was so happy, even though I had gone to the shittiest place just to see a guy. But it was okay because the guy was so amazing."

One of my favorite moments of SLDR life is also the ultimate in hub living: wedding shopping. Not for the gift, but for the date. This works for holidays as well. You scroll through the Palm looking for a suitable date for the occasion. Big wedding? Import. Five days in Los Angeles for business? There must be someone who can fly in for the weekend.

But with the SLDR comes constant and inevitable frustration, because no matter how great the relationship is from a distance, it can never compare to the benefits of a stable, fruitful relationship in your own area code.

Andy: "You know, I just can't seem to meet anyone in New York. Well I can, they just don't live here. I met this great guy, but he lives in Ireland. Then there was someone in Miami. And that guy in Paris. I'd date any one of them, but they are all so far away, so we just e-mail. Why can't I meet anybody here?"

The answer is in his next breath:
"Ah, who cares? It's for the best anyway. I don't have time to deal with it."

If there is a growth category in relationships, the SLDR is most certainly it. It goes back to our poles of influence – travel and communication, both of which allow someone in another hemisphere to remain a daily part of your life.

S "NW"

Paul clicks open an Excel file on his laptop. Up pops several sheets of charts and graphs.

"This is technology at its best," he starts. "I've got the last 13 years on cross-tab."

Indeed he does. There, in a dull glow, are pie charts detailing the national origin of every girl he's slept with. British girls are predominant, followed closely by about seven other euro currency states. Line charts compare the length of the relationship to performance in bed. Other charts tabulate the frequency of vacation hookups relative to those introduced by friends.

On a separate sheet are the data tabs, complete with first names (never last, for privacy), dates, hobbies, preferences, nicknames and fond memories. A composite score ranks the relative success or failure of the relationship. Yes, the hub journal. Seeing the complexity of his analysis, it becomes evident why he was once a successful banker.

"Based on the numbers, I'm not worried," he states.

Aside from a couple of blank entries under the name category, it appears the boy certainly has done his homework. His conclusion that eventually he will meet the right girl is truly backed up by the numbers. There are a couple of relationship 10s, the LDRs that were almost BiMs. There are also a few Sex-in-the-City style entries, the digital equivalent of scratching another notch on the headboard. In between are the rest, a mix of short relationships, regrettable mistakes and dreamy scenarios that didn't work out, for whatever reason.

Regardless, Paul is confident that eventually he will meet the girl who will enable him to stop keeping score on his love life, the girl that will blow away all the others. Hopefully.

Maybe it's fuzzy math – but he figures that if two of 20 relationships were just about there over the last, say, 10 years, then over the next 10 years, even with half the relationships, he's bound to have at least one that will work.

That's why he's not worried. Neither is Shena.

Shena is quickly nearing 40, but like many single women who have never gotten around to getting married she puts up a brave face that masks a depressed ambivalence that comes with staying serially single. She's beautiful. It is nearly impossible to guess her age. Reports show that fully 26% of urban professional women over the age of 35 are in the same category as Shena.

"I'm not worried. When I meet the right guy, it will just happen. If I don't, that's OK too. I have a great life, so why destroy it? The only thing is kids. I want a child. Right now I'm debating, because my two best friends are this gay couple, who also want kids. Should I? Could we share? I'm not sure. It would mean so many changes. I mean, what if they broke up? That would be difficult."

Like everything else, having kids becomes a question of consumption and acquisition. Nothing in life seems to fit the old modes of convention, so why should a family? "Expand your mind," she says. But then they all hesitate because no matter how you slice it, a child between three parents involves quite a big social conditioning step. They can justify it from the materialism point of view, but from the spiritual? That is tougher. Thus, they wait around, biding their time. The idea seems nice ... but rarely is anyone quite ready to put it into practice.

Other single women get around the "no good man" issue by simply having a kid on their own terms, or for both gay couples and single women, adopting. Either way, they feel like they are getting what they want on their own terms, which may be financially more difficult than a traditional relationship, but is preferable to waiting around for the right person to come along out of the blue.

Then there's "the rule". A common safety net for singles all over the urban hubs, a pact made in those moments when S "NW" turns into Single, Worried, usually after a long talk with friends. That's when the deals get made. "OK, we're great friends. We love each other. If I don't find anyone by 30 and you don't either, we'll get married." Later, the number becomes 35, then 40, and you start to plan back ups. I'm not sure what happens after 50, but I have a feeling geriatric versions of Friends, complete with cruise ship season tickets and shuffleboard tournaments, aren't out of the question for 2040.

chapter**nine**

Work it, baby

Of the different lifestyle elements that define hub culture, the first among equals is work if only because work is what most of us spend the majority of the time doing. In hub culture, two kinds of work are shaking out as the dominant models for individual advancement: casual, informal jobs based on personal reputation and networks, and uber-jobs that consume the life of their subjects to such an extent that life doesn't just revolve around work, it is their life. Transecting both are those poles of travel and communication, which affect the way these types of work are approached.

Both work categories are probably evident in broader suburban economies, but their growth appears to be hyper-accelerated in the urban hubs, and in hub culture. Here, individuals may shift between both of these work formats throughout a career, accelerating and downshifting several times over the course of even just a few years. People in the group gain equal experience between the uber-job and the nonjob-job, resulting in a blasé equivalency in our minds. The grass isn't greener on the other side. We know it's the same grass, and everyone keeps hopping the fence to prove it.

The fertilizer on both sides of the fence is travel and communication. On either side, their role and influence are identical: travel is a constant demand fueled by impenetrable restlessness, and communication enables a mental construct that allows individuals to feel like they are master of their own universe, owner of their own network.

Understanding how these two kinds of work are evolving has an impact on the way we think of the hub's individual consumption habits and in terms of the buying hub people do for companies.

In tandem with outsourcing and other trends discussed later, the rise of the uber-job and nonjob-job will cause a realignment of buying power – slowly ebbing out of the traditional "corporation" and into these virtual networks of connected individuals where it flows back and forth between stakeholders inside and outside the company. Those individuals in the uber-jobs outsource their budgets to the nonjobs, and the nonjobs account for decision making across a variety of uber-jobs. Both groups have equal power and both groups must be reached.

Somewhere in the mix is how the group internalizes this work. Again, they say it better than I, so we'll start with the role of mobility, show some insights into the lifestyle and motivations of the nonjob-job, visit an analysis of the uber-job that circulated among the hub culture, and tie it all up with a famous story of self destruction that sums up the angst, arrogance and speed of the new world.

Subject: Back in Ireland
Date: Thursday, 17 May 05:46:48 –0700 (PDT)

Reply | Reply All | Forward | Delete | Previous | Next | Close

> **Hey there, well I'm back in Ireland for the moment and I'm finding it really hard to settle. Any job here just isn't appealing to me. Yesterday I replied to a teaching post in Japan, anything to get away again. I'm teaching now but I'm also just waiting for my two friends in New York to set dates to travel cross–country and if that doesn't happen I'll just go to the west coast instead.**
>
> **Fill me in with any of your news, love always, Leigh.**

I met Leigh in Hong Kong during a long weekend she had taken with a work group of teachers from Dublin, her base city. Dublin may not be a huge hub destination, but it has a young population and a growing reputation as a tech center that bred a community of individuals who fit easily into the hub lifestyle. Like many small countries, people in Ireland think a lot about places outside of Ireland, and a number of Irish have started commuting between the major hubs in an ongoing search for jobs. In so doing they become connected to a growing group of nomadic countrymen who shuttle from hub to hub on different projects.

In turn, they pick up the ideas and trends happening in the hubs and messenger them back to Dublin, which already enjoys increasing turnover from those who simply travel to and from other hubs for leisure or business. A core of Dublin has thus become in tune with the same vibe that is happening elsewhere.

This mobility has changed the way hub troopers view the work process – and syncs well to the companies that are looking for global, mobile workers not tied to living in a particular country. This is one reason why Nick in Melbourne and Leigh in Dublin have so much in common – their paths cross, and since both come from smaller cities, they realize that working in and out of the hubs is critical to their success, regardless of whether or not they stay in a hub for their whole career. If and when they return, they have incubated the way of living and the perspectives, which often include brand awareness and loyalties, that they can then incorporate into their own demand schedules.

Mobility plays a central role in the hub lifestyle. The growing ability for citizens of all countries to cross borders at the drop of a hat for purely professional considerations, or even just the hope of professional opportunities, has tilted the balance of power for attracting A-list workers in favor of multinational companies. Since English remains the language of business, the Irish and Australians benefit particularly.

Asia is a place where hub troopers see opportunity, but the downsides of living in Asian hubs – pollution, distance from family and friends, etc., still make it a bit of a stretch for many in Europe and the Americas to consider as a permanent option. The inability for many Westerners to deal with Asian living is not a significant handicap to their career or even their participation in hub culture, but it does create an advantage for Asians who are comfortable moving between all points on the compass.

Asians used to leave the Asian cities with no intention of returning. Nowadays, Asians commute between these hubs enjoying an edge that comes with understanding the best of East and West. These are the leaders in Tokyo, Shanghai, Singapore and Hong Kong, the people who best embody the hub culture. Not all of them are Asian in ethnic origin, for Asian cities tend to harbor a mix of people who maintain far-flung family connections. Europeans and North Americans (some are the sons and daughters of the 1980s expatriate migrations) raised in Asia's hub cities are starting to realize the same benefits of the East–West understanding and instead of importing Western expertise to Asian markets (as many of their parents did), are finding demand in London, Paris, New York, San Francisco and other markets for their Asian experience.

Rise of the Nonjob-Job

"You're not sure who really has jobs anymore. Everybody seems to get by but nobody goes to work." – Joe

<Miami, Monday afternoon>
"Hello?"

"Hi Rosa ... I'm fine and you. Yes. They won't take seven, the lowest is seven-five, but he is also working eight.

"I know your client wants seven but I can't do that. I took him seven last week and he said no, so I am not going to go back to him now with seven again.

"Mmhmmm.

"The place is great, and the owner has to cover his costs – he doesn't even want to rent anyway. You're lucky he's even considering seven-five. OK, call me back."

Bal Harbour, a mini-Palm Beach, is really nothing more than an upscale shopping center with Versaces and Vuittons and Lacostes nestled amid a number of living and shopping developments a few blocks off the beach. Bal Harbour is one of the most gentrified locations around South Beach and thus a popular spot, especially for those who want to be close to the buzz of South Beach without the trashiness that South Beach actually entails.

Joe lives in Bal Harbour, but only in the loosest sense of the term. His apartment is 3,000 square feet of beachfront condo, recently renovated to dispel the wallpapered and chandeliered opulence of the previous boomer couple. Two low settees, the newest iMAC, and a mattress in the gigantic walk-in closet (itself the average size of a Tokyo apartment) round out the place. A bare giant bed occupies one of the many rooms, glaring white from the bright Miami sun that streams in the open bay windows.

"No curtains, that's why I sleep in the closet. It's so nice and cozy in there."

As if.

He never sleeps in the closet anyway, because to be young and single with money in Miami means that you and your friends are sharing houses and crashing at whichever one is closest to you on any given night. The important thing is that most of your clothes are in one place. For the particular condo in question, the main occupants are the Czech national maids who perform what little cleaning duties need to be done, chiefly laundry, the reason why you need at least your clothes in one place.

On the counter are keys to another apartment on Ocean Drive that is the subject of continuous streams of workmen, sent by the building management to fiddle with little things everyone calls "details." In the real world, such little things are called "shoddy construction-related defects," but in Miami, everything has a certain kind of sweet gloss that makes the constant interruptions and transient apartment squatting go down a little bit easier. Miami is totally sunbelt, and this is a scene that could be repeated easily in LA, or even to some extent Phoenix and Dallas, minus the abundant water. Like everything else in Joe's personal economy, both apartments are an investment, purchased only for the purpose of making money. The term "no fixed address" is not an insult here, and Joe is evocative of many in the hub culture who shift location with the wind. It's tough to reach a 25-year-old guy pulling down $200,000 a year when he's never home and probably doesn't even live at his main fixed address, but he does make a tempting target. Essentially, the place is a giant closet, with some organic orange juice in the fridge and a high-speed DSL connection next to the kitchen sink.

Perpetually for sale. This is how everything is positioned in a market where people get their start on low-margin credit and try to flip a car or a building within the first year. This fits nicely in an attention-deficit economy, where people are absolutely bored with whatever they have from the moment they have it. In America, the big question is how this leveraged sort of living will fare if the general economy continues to tank, or even if it endures a continuous slow slide similar to Japan's post-bubble economy of the 1990s. The answer is: painfully. Everyone thinks he is smarter than the next idiot, and a lot of the day-trading mentality that swept the markets at the turn of the century has now seeped into the broad economy. Thanks to eBay, CNBC and rich overseas friends who can actually afford to do this sort of thing, twenty-something Miami thinks nothing of buying a property, moving in for two months, renovating for six, and moving out when it is sold for a US$50,000 profit the next month. The extra benjis in your pocket allow you to leverage a bigger loan for the next pad, which you will sell for a greater profit while you blow 20% on a few nights out at Nobu Lounge at the Shore Club.

Here you will get to see all your quasi-acquaintances from New York and Rio, in for the weekend, and end up negotiating a deal for the loft apartments that are now available downtown, "the next big area" in 2005.

Like dogs that circle nervously before an earthquake, tradition dictates that when the real-estate people themselves are getting out of all their own properties and bunking down for a rental, it's probably not the best time to buy. But like the weather, even this sell-off is just a summer-time squall. In Miami the hub thinks the old fundamentals don't matter, as there are still plenty of people rolling into town with foreign cash looking to buy up a bit of the boom that lingers in markets like this one, where the broad sector decline hasn't steamrolled traditional forms of quick-money industries, like speculative real estate. The funny thing about Miami is that it's full of models trying to become real-estate brokers, much like Los Angeles used to be full of waiters wanting to become actors. That was back when it was cool to want to be an actor. Now of course, that's all kind of kitsch and the only people who want to be actors work in the New York hotels that haven't yet gone bankrupt.

So Joe, like everyone, tries to buy low and sell high. He'll buy again soon, because there's not much else to do, and besides, "it's just a squall." He's not about to go and find a salaried job at a big anonymous firm. The smartest and most ambitious people in the hub generation have concluded that the way to make serious money is not necessarily tied to a standard corporate job. It is now about exploiting gaps that exist between big companies.

Joe owns three apartments in the Miami area and became a broker in Miami after dropping out of NYU. He's 25. His parents are from one of those little towns up the Florida coast that people moved to back when the American suburbs were considered a desirable concept instead of a roll-curbed prison. Like Ruben, Rebecca and the others, his response was to bolt to the city as soon as he could, to multitask his life in an attempt to get as many experiences in as he can, while he is young, cute and confident enough to get away with it.

Multitasking is how the new people work, and the mix with leisure is mandatory, which is one reason why Miami remains ground-center as one of the hottest places in the world to be living right now. People want the lifestyle; their work is only a means of achieving a certain lifestyle.

<Back to Bal Harbour>
Walk through the darkly tinted double doors of Neiman Marcus into an empty cavernous location called the department store. It is eerily silent and totally vacant. March straight through cosmetics, stopping for a squirt of Acqua di Parma, and loiter, waiting for the elevator.

Ping. Doors open.

Glide up two levels, admiring the vast silent display of men's and ladies' wear from the rounded glass capsule, with mental note to check out the leather loafers next to that mannequin. Straighten T-shirt. Doors open. Time for business.

Enter Zodiac, lunch. It's small, it's packed, and poor (according to her name tag) Sheila has to listen to the same conversations day in and day out while she peers out her giant glasses at the ladies who lunch and the guys who sell while she dishes out from a wooden basket extra potato bread that comes in a little popover with the chicken consommé.

She quietly rolls her eyes at the scene before her.

"You still have 15 days to pull out of the Continuim. I mean, you should at least check out Aqua, I think it's more your style."

Joe is at work. He's chatting to an elegant, classic-featured guy who looks about the same age, sitting with an older Latin woman of refined simplicity. They just plopped $1.1 million into a new development at the bottom of South Beach with a rival agent. It turns out that Joe's brother is studying at Columbia with this guy, which means that before the day is over, an entire group of Columbia students will be inadvertently cutting a $1.5 million real-estate deal in Miami by simply mentioning that "Continuim is over" when one of them calls to tell him about the Man Ray party in the city that he just missed.

"The only problem is, I would love to look at Aqua if you really think it's worth a look, but I'm going to Spain tomorrow before I return to school. Maybe my mother can go." The Latin guy adjusts himself as he finishes the last of the Cobb salad in front of him and eventually settles lightly against the back of the chair. The woman with him turns out to be his mother, and she studies Joe slowly, then confirms that she would be willing to look.

Nevermind that Aqua is a giant construction zone on a causeway in North Beach with only a walk-in showroom and a few Bathaulp fixtures in a mock kitchen to show for it, Joe has told her about Aqua's grand plans, and she knows she's not buying based on appearances, she is buying on momentum and on trust. True enough, six months later Aqua at Allison Island was nearly sold out.

"The editor of *Architectural Digest* just bought there. It's much more artistic than anything else out there and it will be just like owning your own deco building, only new. There's a model facing east that was designed by Harare and Hari, you know, the famous architects. There are a few other architects who did something there too. I think they are Iranian, Hare and Harari. Anyway, they're in *Wallpaper** all the time."

Joe takes a bite of his chicken, which has arrived and grown cold, owing to the fact that he just did more work in 10 minutes than he would have done all day sitting on the cell trying to negotiate the other deal with Rosa.

Speaking of … the Mercedes-Benz-branded Motorola begins to vibrate across the table. (The phone came standard with the SL500.)

"Hi Rosa. Yes he's still at seven-five.

"What would motivate them at seven? Well I think seven-five would motivate them.

"OK, talk soon. Thanks, bye."

The phone flips closed and Joe's mind returns to the couple at the next table, even though he is crouched against the table facing his agent-partner. He speaks low as he shovels salad. "Latin banking money. Ecuador. What banks are there in Ecuador? I think she has six million from the sale of their other places. They just need a place to park for awhile, so who cares if it's 1.1 at Continium or 1.5 million at Aqua". (In economic terms, he means that price is not the issue here.)

Joe's associate, who has been sitting there taking it all in, nods and stares at the pastel prints behind his head, studying the grays and pinks and greens that cover most of South Florida for any indication of originality, finding none. His eyes roam the wall, then focus back and he says: "They'll double their money in two years if they do Aqua. It's a no-miss scenario. They can't go wrong. Do you think they can come by today?" The eyes shift down to a fork picking at flaky crab cake, and he thumbs his Nokia as he casually scrolls through his missed-call list.

Joe flips back to the Latin mother, flashing his biggest smile. "Great.

I'll call you and we can go check it out." She nods, and looks at him, sizing him up. "Yes it is settled then. I will come and view it after Carlos goes to New York." She stands to depart and gives him a warm, if perhaps a little wary, hug.

It's not like these guys are dishonest. The art of the hub deal is based on a certain kind of integrity that employs a sense of fatalism combined with systematic optimism. On one hand the market is going down and everybody is offloading so they can pick up more when the market is low, making it hard for a person to say a buyer is going to make money on the property with a straight face. On the other hand they figure today's buyers have their reasons for picking up, and that (especially in luxury Miami real estate) there aren't many suckers.

So everybody's a winner and you just worry about your own reasons, letting everyone else sort out their own. Ah, the market. But the fact remains that luxury Miami real estate is not going to last much longer than the cycle in the rest of the US market, meaning slow growth in the foreseeable future. Growth rates of 25%+ a year common throughout urban markets like Miami are a thing of the past, and a collective denial exists in the hubs about the risk of consumer and mortgage debt – no one thinks that a slow US economy will short circuit his ability to afford the latest SLK.

Despite that undercurrent of impending doom, and even when everybody is not a winner, a person that sells anything in the JOE economy tends to put the vestige of honesty and integrity forward as a sort of Holy Grail, because he realizes that reputation is everything. The moment somebody gets burned on a deal or in some way is victimized by a business transaction that you have helped initiate or broker, you are finished.

So in essence, what IS the Joe economy? Above all, it's a liberal arts degree. In practice, it starts with a disdain for big corporations, but the need to leverage them in deals. The Joe economy continues with individualized business propositions fueled by a reliance on honesty and networks to make money, generally through the offer of service – real estate, design, consulting. It peaks with a refusal to be associated with anything smelly, and concludes with an involuntary focus on veneer – in conversation, in life, in work, and in determinations of what works and what doesn't, in an attempt to gloss-up life to look better for potential clients.

The hubs realize the value of their personal, individual brand, and will stop at nothing to build and maintain a positively shiny reputation. In this world, anonymity does not exist, and an angry or irate client can do more damage with one well-placed e-mail than a lifetime of lunchtime schmoozing at Neiman Marcus can ever repair. As transparency in communication increases, we'll see an even tighter allegiance to this ideal among those who seek to remain competitive, because it is harder to hide than ever before. People trust honest people. On the other hand, desperation is a powerful motivating factor, and a prolonged period of tough global times will make the art of the deal all the more artful, undoubtedly.

So in the hubs these nonjob jobs rest on three fundamentals: a disdain for normal 9-5 work, utter faith in networking as your main job skill, and a reliance on an honest reputation to negotiate deals, from which you derive a high (if sporadic) standard of living. Since big companies are accounting for fewer and fewer global jobs, the JOE economy is bypassing the old corporate paths to power by opting to build its own virtual networks. These networks are defined not by geography and proximity as much as by social compatibility and lifestyle, which lead to economic opportunity.

The wider hub people cast their network nets, the more likely they are to find gaps and opportunities that they can exploit for financial gain, because governments and bigger businesses tend to move slower than the people who make up the hub. Lack of information, combined with lack of individual trust and relationships, may hamper fluidity in the economy, but it is a fertile ground in which many people who work to build these relationships find economic opportunity. The hubs realize that the more central they are to transactions in these relationships, the more they can maximize these opportunities.

The value of reputation and the time and effort spent in cultivating the "individual career" cause pause for thought for marketers who operate on the idea that most people are motivated and defined primarily by their work, and that their economic spending power is determined not just by their salary but by the purchase power held by their position within a company. This is relevant to individual consumption levels and purchasing power, but is also interesting from the much larger corporate spending point of view.

Purchase decision-making is a major criterion by which marketers decide whom to select to receive sales and marketing messages, and it is typically defined by business-to-business (corporate) buying, which accounts for up to two thirds of broad economic output. As more individuals opt for careers that leave them out of the corporate loop, and conversely, as large companies continue to pare their work forces to razor thin levels run by armies of outsourced specialists, the proportion of purchase decision-making by large and established companies is ebbing in favor of informal networks of individuals who have more ethereal buying power, centered outside the actual target company. This makes influencing the real decision-makers difficult to achieve and even harder to manipulate because it is spread more widely. It is tough to reach the full potential audience of your buyers: they just aren't at work anymore. Therefore, a marketing strategy that simply targets the decision-makers in large corporations can be inadequate.

But you can reach and influence this group of people by creating corporate buying messages that appeal to their sense of independence and this innate desire to manage their own image. If a product or service is positioned as assisting them in their work, to shorten time spent or to simplify a process, they see direct relevance to them. This direct relevance makes it possible for them to act as a product ambassador, and enables you to reach a wider swath of decision-makers responsible for buying decisions about your product.

Rise of the Uber-job

"I don't do enough." – Natalia, Hong Kong

The second group in the hub-culture job scene is the uber-worker, the people who enable companies to continue downsizing without sacrificing productivity, because they will always do more to make sure they are not the ones downsized. She is the corporate achiever who is so driven that she feels she has to work 12 hours a day to be validated, partly because the demand of work dictates that she does so, and partly because she might self-destruct if not for the pressure of work to keep her in line.

Much of hub culture is filled with this group of global professionals who are consumed by work and use it as a distraction from other things not happening in their life – whether it's relationships (hello S "NW") or just a well rounded sense of balance.

A great article appeared in the *Financial Times* about this very subject. The author's words struck a cord and were picked up and forwarded among many people in urban professional settings around the world, producing yet another cult commentary for hub culture:

Subject: Work It
Date: Tuesday, 04 June, 08:16:44 +9:00 GMT

Reply | Reply All | Forward | Delete | Previous | Next | Close

Pls. read. This was sent to me before but I only read it now. I think this is so true. Especially when I was a hair-dresser on fire for my dad. Working late and insane stress gave me complete self-validation. That's Manila. NRV

FRONT PAGE – WEEKEND FT: Today's generation of high-earning professionals maintain that their personal fulfillment comes from their jobs and the hours they work. They should grow up, says Thomas Barlow, *Financial Times*.

... the idea has grown up, in recent years, that work should not be just a means to an end, a way to make money, support a family, or gain social prestige–but should provide a rich and fulfilling experience in and of itself. Jobs are no longer just jobs; they are lifestyle options.

Recruiters at financial companies, consultancies and law firms have promoted this conception of work. Job advertisements promise challenge, wide experiences, opportunities for travel and relentless personal development.

Michael is a 33–year–old management consultant who has bought into this vision of late–20th century work. Intelligent and well–educated – with three degrees, including a doctorate – he works in Munich, and has a "stable, long–distance relationship" with a woman living in California. He takes 140 flights a year and works an average of 80 hours a week. Some weeks he works more than 100 hours. When asked if he likes his job, he will say, "I enjoy what I'm doing in terms of the intellectual challenges." Although he earns a lot, he doesn't spend much.

He rents a small apartment, though he is rarely there, and has accumulated very few possessions. He justifies the long hours not in terms of wealth acquisition, but solely as part of a "learning experience." This attitude to work has several interesting implications, mostly to do with the shifting balance between work and non-work, employment and leisure.

Because fulfilling and engrossing work – the sort that is thought to provide the most intense learning experience – often requires long hours or captivates the imagination for long periods of time, it is easy to slip into the idea that the converse is also true: that just by working long hours, one is also engaging in fulfilling and engrossing work. This leads to the popular fallacy that you can measure the value of your job (and, therefore, the amount you are learning from it) by the amount of time you spend on it.

And, incidentally, when a premium is placed on learning rather than earning, people are particularly susceptible to this form of self-deceit.

Thus, whereas in the past, when people in their 20s or 30s spoke disparagingly about nine-to-five jobs it was invariably because they were seen as too routine, too unimaginative, or too bourgeois. Now, it is simply because they don't contain enough hours. Young professionals have not suddenly developed a distaste for leisure, but they have solidly bought into the belief that a 45-hour week necessarily signifies an unfulfilling job...

Such is the character of the modern, international professional, at least throughout his or her 20s. Spare time, goods and relationships, these are all willingly traded for the exigencies of work. Nothing is valued so highly as accumulated experience. Nothing is neglected so much as commitment. With this work ethic – or perhaps one should call it a "professional development ethic" – becoming so powerful, the globally mobile generation now in its late 20s and early 30s has garnered considerable professional success.

For many, it is a trap that is difficult to break out of, not least because they are so caught up in a culture of professional development. And spoilt for choice, some become paralyzed by their opportunities, unable to do much else in their lives, because they are so determined not to let a single one of their chances slip. If that means minimal personal commitments well into their 30s, so be it ...

[They] grew up as part of a generation with fewer social constraints determining their futures than has been true for probably any other generation in history. They were taught at school that when they grew up they could "do anything," "be anything." It was an idea that was reinforced by popular culture, in films, books and television.

The notion that one can do anything is clearly liberating. But life without constraints has also proved a recipe for endless searching, endless questioning of aspirations. It has made this generation obsessed with self–development and determined, for as long as possible, to minimize personal commitments in order to maximize the options open to them.

One might see this as a sign of extended adolescence. Eventually, they will be forced to realize that living is as much about closing possibilities as it is about creating them.

No adequate response to Barlow's criticism of the motivations that surround the uber-job group can ignore the fact that he makes these people out to be norman-no-mates, consumed by themselves. Or that he thinks this group needs to grow up. He's only right to an extent.

There's also nothing wrong with high expectations and demands for yourself and your environment. It's all about experiencing that perfect life, no matter how overdriven you have to be to push yourself to it. But the motivating factor remains the quest for satisfaction, that spiritual contentment which the vapid materialism that surrounds us isn't delivering. The desire to race through professional life distracts the group from that larger search for spiritual peace, but that's good, because no one's sure about how to find spiritual contentment anyway.

That said, it is also about survival. The practical reason people work outrageous hours and spend all their time revolving around work is that there is a dull throb in the back of the brain that reminds us if we don't, someone else will. And nobody, despite the initial glee following a professional derailment, really wants to spend life job-hunting out of a neighborhood coffee shop. It is the defining fear among the tribe to experience a mid-thirties or mid-twenties disappearance from the social fabric of work that anchors so much identity in hub life.

You can alternate between uber-job and nonjob job, and everyone does at some point or the other, but the idea of giving up either or both for all that other stuff is like asking hunting dogs not to chase a fox. Besides, with everything that's going on, people can barely handle their careers, let alone a rewarding home life.

Sometimes, people can't even handle their career. The group watches in mock horror as the occasional stink bomb works its way through the electronic network, a Grimm Fairy Tale of caution that reminds the group how perilous and insecure their uber-job can be. Torpedoes can strike from any direction – the big merger, another round of corporate layoffs, misfired political backstabbing, unplanned pregnancy …

Occasionally, there is even an accidental corporate suicide. Executed in public, everyone huddles like kids around a campfire, mouths ajar, eyes wide, fully contributing to a professional equivalent of a slow motion town square hanging, all with a few clicks of the keyboard and the forward function:

Subject: Fw: Life in Private Equity – The Mega Stud Version
Date: Thursday, May 24, 10:18:55 –1200 EST

Reply | Reply All | Forward | Delete | Previous | Next | Close

As you may know, the only person more arrogant than an investment banker is someone in private equity. Investment bankers pride themselves on making vast amounts of money, but a successful private equity professional takes devilish pride and supports an even bigger ego for working fewer hours while making even more money than his (rarely her) investment banking brethren.

Unfortunately, some members of the private equity community mistakenly believe that their growing wealth is the result of their own talent and charming personality rather than a simple profiting from the hoarding of capital, as Karl Marx so astutely described.

Consider the plight of Peter Chung (see attached e-mail), a recent hire at the Carlyle Group ... as of May 15, Chung alluded to having had sexual relations with five "hot chicks." According to Chung's own calculations, there are roughly one billion "hot chicks" remaining in Korea. Clearly there is a break in Chung's sexual predator model as he apparently believes that not only is the global female population of three billion comprised of one-third hot Korean chicks, but he will be able to sleep with that many before his finest member falls off or he dies of exhaustion. Sadly, Chung cannot complete his mission alone. The quality of prophylactics in Korea are not quite up to US standards (Chung would probably claim Korean condoms are too small) and he needs your help to continue his quest for infamy. If you would like to contribute to this valiant mission, please direct your gift of FDA-approved "domes" to the address below:

Peter Chung
The Carlyle Group
Suite 1009, CCMM Bldg.
12, Yoido-dong, Youngdeungpo-ku
Seoul 150-010, Korea

Chung asks that you consider using FedEx or another international overnight courier since he may be on the verge of running out of protection.

Alternatively, if you would like to pursue a job working for The Carlyle Group in Korea, write to the following address:

The Honorable James A. Baker
1001 Pennsylvania Avenue NW
Suite 220 South
Washington, DC 20004-2505

Please note that Mr. Baker, the lead spokesperson for The Carlyle Group, is the former Secretary of State from the George Herbert Walker Bush Administration. Since leaving the White House, Jim Baker has continued his international mission to spread goodwill and STDs throughout the world by supporting young Romeos such as Mr. Chung.

For a first-hand account of life in private equity, please read Peter Chung's travelogue (attached). Please keep in mind that Chung's experience is partially a function of his prior status as a "stud" and may not be reflective of private equity experiences in general. Not all of us can hope to be as smart, debonair and modest as Mr. Chung.

Regards,

Justin

From: Peter Chung
Subject: LIVING LIKE A KING
Date: Tue, 15 May, 17:26:21 −0700

Reply | Reply All | Forward | Delete | Previous | Next | Close

So I've been in Korea for about a week and a half now and what can I say, LIFE IS GOOD.

I've got a spanking brand new 2000 sq. foot three-bedroom apt. with a 200 sq. foot terrace running the entire length of my apartment with a view overlooking Korea's main river and nightline ... Why do I need three bedrooms? Good question, ... the main bedroom is for my queen size bed, ...where CHUNG is going to fuck every hot chick in Korea over the next two years (five down, 1,000,000,000 left to go) ... the second bedroom is for my harem of chickies, and the third bedroom is for all of you fuckers when you come out to visit my ass in Korea. I go out to Korea's finest clubs, bars and lounges pretty much every other night on the weekdays and everyday on the weekends too (I think in about two months, after I learn a little bit of the buyside business I'll probably go out every night on the weekdays). I know I was a stud in NYC but I pretty much get about, on average, five to eight phone numbers a night and at least three hot chicks who say that they want to go home with me every night I go out.

I love the buyside ... I have bankers calling me everyday
with opportunities and they pretty much cater to my
every whim – you know (golfing events, lavish dinners, a
night out clubbing). The guys I work with are also all chill
– I live in the same apt building as my VP and he drives me
around in his Porsche (one of three in all of Korea) to
work and when we go out. What can I say ... life is good ...
CHUNG is KING of his domain here in Seoul ...

So, all of you fuckers better keep in touch and start
making plans to come out and visit my ass ASAP, I'll show
you guys an unbelievable time ... My contact info is
below ... Oh, by the way ... someone's gotta start
fedexing me boxes of domes, I brought out about 40 but
I think I'll run out of them by Saturday ...

Laters,
CHUNG

Of course, this particular story eventually made its way into the popular press, and became a hub legend of instant reference, a cautionary tale from the crypt of unemployment, which subsequently ensued for the poor Mr. Chung. For, needless to say, the Carlyle Group were not ecstatic about the contents of the e-mail, and promptly took action against its new employee by firing him.

So many things about this particular bit of culture vomit are evocative of the hub culture. First you have the global nature of the communication, with address strings that include contacts between the big banks, media, consulting and lots of people in between, a network of forwards that ensure everyone got this e-mail over a certain period of a few weeks. It took only three days to bounce from Seoul to New York, and from there to London, Hong Kong and Tokyo – locations from which I received various versions between the original send date of May 17th and my receipt on May 21st. Even more interesting is the conversation it sparked, with various rants by senders such as Justin, who was just one of a long stream of disgusted commentators.

There is the relationship angle, which so neatly fits into the S "NW" box of relationships, if perhaps expressed a bit more crudely than the first example. There is the brand management angle, so embarrassingly relevant to the Carlyle Group, that highlights how the most random and insignificant image incident can become a global news story in a matter of days, even hours.

There is even the proximity angle. Late one night on the way back to Delhi from Agra, I mentioned the story to a woman I met traveling and she blurted: "Oh my god, Peter Chung? I have these friends in New York who went to high school with him! He was so embarrassed."

And finally, there is poor Peter himself, who has the ironic satisfaction of global notoriety, but at the cost of his hub reputation. The woman wondered if he changed his name.

chapter**ten**

Anonymous Proximity

Proximity and anonymity. Much of hub living is based on selectively choosing when to deploy force fields of these two concepts, from a social point of view. Even though the hub group is wildly diverse and global in scale and perspective, the universal tie-in it shares is based on common cultural influences and personalities. Those common icons can vary greatly by the moment, or the group you are with. To some, the universal tie-in may be a labor activist in social justice circles, for others it may be a rogue trader in the financial world. Somewhere out there is even someone who still finds sheepish delight in telling his dinner party guests that he once knew Peter Chung.

Conversations among hub influentials often dwell on these networks of influence, and include a parlor game of measuring who has access to tap into these different networks. People use it for establishing perceived status and to intellectually mark their terrain.

<Sushi Republic. Wednesday night, Miami Beach>
Trey announces that his friend Nora is moving to Dubai. Nora, it turns out, has been employed by a Saudi prince and financial trader who made and lost a fortune during the global Internet boom.

"Talk about a dream job …" gushes the group.

Trey relates her typical day: planning the prince's evening social events, which often includes elaborate Miami parties for hundreds of Palm Beach luminaries – the models, foreigners, and entertainment creatures who call Miami home at least a few weekends a year. Nora accompanies the prince on his travels, along with the phalanx of security guards and a resident DJ. The resident DJ is, by the way, the ultimate hub elite accessory, spinning in the tradition of private cooks and manicurists that symbolized super-elite status in the 1980s and 1990s. What could be more niche-modern: someone to manage your entertainment consumption.

Trey uses this information about Nora to massage his perception among the others in his group. Since he has no relation to the prince whatsoever, it has no personal relevance to him or the people he is with except as an anecdote that makes everyone feel closer to the prince, somehow validating their own stature. The final, subconscious conclusion is that, by degree, they all travel in the same circles as the prince. This is cultural proximity.

Since the prince has no real direct relevance to their lives, the consequences of it not being true are also minimal, mitigating the fact that Trey probably heard whatever he knows through a convolution of sources that are half right. In Trey's quest to build and manage his own personal brand, he picks up on that random fact and this tidbit of information, then uses it to position himself with regard to the rest of the group.

There is no animosity in it, and he has incentive to be right about what he says to maintain his credibility, which, just as in professional life, is vastly important. He does in fact turn the prince into a product for his own use, and further groups societal icons and landmarks to anchor the worldview he projects toward the others.

On a macro level, this desire for proximity to things we know is what drives growth in sponsorship as an effective marketing tool. By tapping into someone famous with a product, consumers come to identify your product with something that can be theirs, for a price. They subsequently adopt the product as a proxy for their relationship with something well known. From a shoe manufacturer's sponsorship of athletes to the casual linking of yourself to famous personalities, the hub markets itself individually while it absorbs the messages of icons it tries to identify with. The thinking goes, if you buy the shoes, you get a piece of the king, which makes you the king of your little universe. If you shop where Nicole Kidman shops, you get a bit of her glamour.

Another feature of cultural proximity pops up with the tendency for new trends seen among the super elite – stars and athletes and business or political figures – anyone in the public consciousness – to first seep into the hub, creating a wider audience for previously stratospheric concepts. This is true with many hot categories, such as the rise of spas, a previously stars-only concept that filtered out to the hubs, and additionally to mass markets. Essentially, anything considered exclusive or rare can eventually be positioned for the hubs to consume, provided it appears to be something they are receiving first. This is part of why major product launches (the BMW 7 series for example) premiere across several hub cities simultaneously – London, New York and Tokyo. A two-week delay can cause "severe" emotional distress. Even the most silly new concepts in health, like oxygen bars, first develop in hubs.

The quest for proximity, however non-tangible, also drives much of the hub's fascination with "hot" restaurants and nightclubs. Unlike the masses who would logically go to a place for the food or good prices, the hubs choose to frequent the glass world of haute-anything because they see themselves as part of the same quixotic culture that includes the stars, who may shine a little brighter, but are just a sideshow in their own little acting scenario. This, not the food, is a little bit of the reason for success behind people like Alain Ducasse.

The very presence of the hub in these "hot" locations supports a business, creating demand for more such products, and driving architects and restaurant founders to create their projects for the consumption of the hub, using stars as bait. They make money from the hub's fascination with itself, not the hub's fascination with the stars who may be sitting at the next table. It is a completely narcissistic viewpoint, but probably more personally satisfying than living vicariously through celebrities, as seems to be the case with "May I have your autograph?" mass culture.

Hub members refuse to associate lust for proximity with "star fucking" (an oft-used hub term to describe people who are overly into the machinations of celebrity) because they are too worried about their own quest to make themselves into a star of their own network, however micro. Hub culture further acknowledges stars as a foreign or unreachable concept. But then it endeavors to adopt lifestyle strategies to increase its proximity to that glamorized lifestyle – so you feel like a star, even for a moment, even if you're so not. When hub creatures view the stars and super-influential as within reach, they tend to mimic cultural attitudes the stars may espouse. Proximity creates the market that the stars supposedly so influence, almost by accident. This is why star culture is worshipped by marketers who think nothing of paying US$5 million+ for celebrity sponsorships. But marketers must understand, it's not about the star, it's about the hub.

The drive for proximity in conversations and interactions with friends and associates is a defining characteristic of hub culture: people want to control their surroundings, and that includes their image as an element within those surroundings. They will use any tool at their disposal, whether Prada backpack or "inside story," not for the others, but for themselves.

Watch how the hub uses this.

Wishing to escape the pressures of the star-studded life, an NBA player buys an enormous house under an assumed name in a quiet, exclusive part of a hub city. He does it under an alias to avoid attracting attention and in hopes of avoiding the party scene that haunts his normal life. He figures that the area would be the safest place to escape.

Days after moving in his illusion of privacy is shattered when helicopters and police descend on the neighborhood to execute one of the largest drug busts in local history ... at the neighbor's house. Nice, and so much for anonymity when the attendant TV crews discovered who actually lived next door. All of this was of little consequence to anyone, except for the agent who got wind of the story when the NBA star subsequently tried to sell the house. While respecting the confidentiality of the client, he couldn't resist the opportunity to share the information with those in his own circle, in his attempt to leverage his proximity to the star among his group of friends and contacts.

In that sense, information has become very refined by constant packaging, leaving the hub to spend lots of time reading between the lines. We gauge the truth in series of statements that are so vague and blasé that it's hard to tell what is real and what isn't. Everybody knows everything, and to some extent everyone, through someone else. And everyone loves a good story, so long as it can't be linked back if it is untrue gossip.

Since the group is constantly searching for its own proximity and connections, much of what gets said is quickly adopted and taken as fact with little analysis or look at what is behind the reasoning for such a conclusion. When it has to do with stars, everyone knows it is meaningless anyway – it is much more about having that glow rub off so that you can command more influence or power on your home turf. Since the landmarks of good proximity constantly change, so the stories do as well. This makes hub stories very transient, valuable only for the light impression they leave that influences their audience about the value and association of their favorite brand: themselves.

Like many aspects of high culture, the assumed-name situation employed by the NBA star reflects seepage to the hub, which brings us to the flip side of proximity, which is anonymity. Anonymity is the attempt to create walls between aspects of our public life, a manufactured, proxi-privacy. In what could be termed as irony, this very quest for anonymity stems from the desire for proximity in the sense that anonymity is a trend that ebbed out from the stars, who have been pursuing a glamorized form of it for years. It's only recently that the general population has felt necessary to pursue the same goal with such fervor. It is sought because so much of hub culture has become transparent and small, leaving nowhere to hide. The hubs offer visibility and identity when your network is global and everyone knows you by reputation. This keeps the hub in line, but also suffocates.

The release valve is a mirage, but it's better than nothing. In response to the spotlight of the network, both professional and social, the hub tries to chop and sort life by creating a form of multiple personality. It has special application for the digital world, where years of assumed identities online are seeping deep into the cultural fabric. We are becoming masters of the multiple identity, and we are beginning to forget how to separate truth from fiction at the same time we develop expertise in managing co-existing personas that are largely separate.

It's obvious everywhere – from the now natural method of giving a false name for restaurant reservations to the use of multiple legal names for different accounts – especially between countries and bank accounts – not quite fraud but certainly a sophisticated effort to protect privacy. At the same time that the digital elite are screaming about the online multitudes losing their privacy, new screens of privacy are springing up in face-to-face society at an ever faster rate. The social screens we employ are designed to protect us from the necessity of interaction with anyone who is not pre-selected, pre-screened and rubber-stamped beforehand. And when you do have to interact with them (whoever "them" is), what is presented is so altered that it is impossible for the service providers to know very much about the real person.

This is largely with respect to the hub's interactions with those who serve in a physical manner – from desk clerks in hotels to the restaurants that cater to the discreet reservation. The backdoor exit. The private room. The velvet rope. All separate the hub from whatever is "out there." Even without these guards, the screening system for selective anonymity marches onward, all the way to the random person you may have just met at the bar with your friends, where you create a false sense of who you are to keep him at bay, and often, where you embellished or lied outright about who you are or what you do, just for a joke, or to maintain your comfort level of anonymity. This continual deception glosses everything, making the outside veneer of urban life impossibly bright, moneyed and slick, to the point that many in the hub actually start to believe their own story, however true or not.

The growth of multiple identities within the hub is also a function of our ongoing ability to reinvent our personalities through the Internet and digital communication, or to manage several personas among several unrelated groups in the real world. This capacity to reinvent ourselves in a stream of constant chat and to show different faces to different people is silent and transparent, and certainly below the surface of our conversation with established networks on the "public" level, where we work and play with our existing, so carefully screened, networks.

But with the intensity of hub life and the ability to escape it at the drop of a hat, today's urban dweller finds it pretty easy indeed to juggle multiple interests, multiple sets of friends and largely parallel lifestyles – certainly online, but increasingly in different cities, whether it's London to Barcelona, New York to Miami, or Hong Kong to Bangkok. Importantly, this is even true within bigger cities themselves, where individual personas may be altered from one group to the other, and never shall the two groups cross, fingers crossed. This means Tuesday can be urban goth intellectual night, while Friday is Latin tango lesson night.

Sometimes it backfires – and worlds collide when unexpected connections pop up, as they invariably do because everyone is out looking for their anonymous little secrets. This just fuels even grander attempts to break out of the perceived network and dip into a subculture that differs from the existence of your proximate reality. Is this behind the resurgence in "Eyes-Wide-Shut" swing clubs? I jest, sort of.

Online, the ability to assume new identities reaches its zenith:

Miss Vapor: you busy?
Jock28:   sup. not really u.
Miss Vapor: Not much, just hanging. Long day at work, nothing on tv
Jock28:   cool. where ru.

Miss Vapor:	Kensington. U?
Jock28:	Docklands
Miss Vapor:	lots of people moving in down there. U have flatmates?
Jock28:	yep. absolute wank. U?
Miss Vapor:	no live alone. I did but she kept using my stuff without asking.
Jock28:	stats?
Miss Vapor:	Look, I'm not here to hook up I'm just here to chat.
Jock28:	Cool. Just asking. stats?
Miss Vapor:	26, 5.8, 130, swf. U?
Jock28:	28, 6.2, 185, brn/blue. you do what?
Miss Vapor:	I'm in trading. I import Asian antiques and furniture from Bali. U?
Jock28:	Cool. Trader. I'm a trader too. But banking.

Tony2touch:	Hey wassup.
Miss Vapor:	Hi. I'm fine.
Tony2touch:	What u up to?
Miss Vapor:	Relaxation. Looking for a movie partner.
Tony2touch:	the thrill of random encounter?
Miss Vapor:	Something like that. What r u into?
Tony2touch:	I could be into a movie. Do you have a pic?
Miss Vapor:	Sure. I'll email it to you. Send me yours. Then maybe we can meet.
Tony2touch:	Hot. Sending now. I clicked on your profile. Nice you are doctor for real?
Miss Vapor:	Of course darling. So who do u model for?
Tony2touch:	Ok sent.
Tony2touch:	What kind of doctor.
Miss Vapor:	Does it matter?

The circumstances may vary slightly, but three factors have enabled this selective anonymization: the sheer size of today's urban populations, which enables you to regularly jump tracks, a growing willingness to meet people online (especially from circles of already existing contacts), and a wider need for people to multitask their lives as a result of rapidly changing jobs, mobility and varied demands on time.

chaptereleven
XTREME Leisure

Red Bull: "Are you going to play tonight?"
Hare: "I'm playing. See you on the slopes."

They Love the Nightlife
\<Midtown Manhattan, Tuesday night\>
Depending on what you're into, New York is the definition of proximity. The heat generated by the beautiful confluence of money, celebrity and sex makes this city the brightest shining hub of hub culture. Everyone pays homage, and here, leisure reaches its most sophisticated level of development in the nightlife, where materialism and consumption fall into ridges of acceptance. It's Tuesday and the bright young things who call the city home are out and about, having successfully dodged the bridge-and-tunnel set by staying in for the weekend. Friday nights in many cities are now considered bridge-and-tunnel, and the people who populate popular perception generally steer clear of public locations unless it's a special event.

But it's Tuesday, and for this moment, which is by definition SO over the minute it's said, it's a familiar routine: Cherry at the W Tuscany for cocktails, followed by The Park, located in the Meat Packing District, followed by Lotus, the It place of the moment. Helen is ready. A perfect example of New York grrrl, she has bounced from job to job since graduating from school in Washington. The half Korean, half American epitomizes the New York scene: ethnic, with roots that extend into several communities, demanding complete control of the New York moment. The radar is finely tuned, and her ability to sniff death of a trend, a restaurant, a color, anything, is eclipsed only by her loyalty to something she truly likes, which is nothing, except her friends.

Like most of the people in this global group, she is studiously ambivalent. Any trend or fashion idea or restaurant is defined first by who else is there. If the friends are there or if the social/networking/buzzy vibe is present, then it is deemed acceptable. No vibe, no Helen. No pre-buzz, no Helen. I say pre-buzz because by the time the buzz actually hits Helen and her crew are usually past it, concerned that they may get caught standing next to the rotting carcass of yesterday's "it" concept.

In the professional sense, she is currently nonjob, less concerned with working 15 hour days than she was two years ago, when she had the uber-job job. Some would call a lifestyle of living from cocktails to lunch a thinly veiled career exaltation of socialite life. And that coupled with a value system arranged around elite consumerism, is a shallow one at that. But these are the same people who don't know a Manolo Blahnik from a Cappellini. You be the judge. But in all that "itness" there is a lust for beauty and comfort that defines some aspect of identity, our feelings about ourselves and the way we see ourselves in the world. These people are not dumb and blindly materialistic, or even shallow, which is a common response people give when they see beautiful urban things on the play. They are demanding and obsessed with the appearance of class and propriety. In the end it might have some negative effects on the ability to maintain a holistic sense of spiritual enlightenment, but it makes a nice substitute.

<Arrival at Cherry, 7 p.m. Helen, BJ and Andrew>
Helen: "I hope you're not bored."

"So I thought we'd go to Park tonight, it's this little restaurant downtown, and we could maybe get something to eat there and then go elsewhere for a drink." (It's all about the understatement, as at the moment The Park is the hottest restaurant in Meat Packing, which still holds a claim as a hot section of the city.)

Drinks are quaffed in the dark light of Cherry, a deep dark bar situated in midtown at the W Tuscany. Cherry borrows influences from the much hyped global urban aesthetic and features several now standard elements of the new modernism, first defined by Philippe Starck and Ian Schrager when they did their series of hip hotels. The funny thing about Ws is that everyone knows they are an attempt to cash in on the look of hub culture, which makes them not-quite-there. Almost though. Good try. Owned by Starwood,

W was the first to discover that everyone was absolutely bored with floral carpets and dingy walls in the legions of formerly high-class hotels that were eerily standard – the Hyatts and Sheratons of the world.

But people don't care that W is a knockoff. As an overplayed concept and even though people roll their eyes dramatically and say "it's a chain" when you mention it, Starwood has done a great job of bringing the global design vibe to mainstream middle-aged business guys. They did it by taking cues from the design and brand leaders like Starck and offering it up to the Helens of the world as a slightly more accessible option. The middle-aged suits always follow.

So the result is that people still swish into W lobbies, past the Japanese bamboo or the chain mail or the highly lacquered furniture, feeling like they are someplace that while not necessarily uber, is certainly superior.

The same with their bars like Cherry, where the chaise longue, modeled after the Mondrian's famous mattress (where beautiful hub-trotting LA people spent the late '90s lying around sipping Sky Bar martinis) dominates the room. At Cherry the staff all meet the "B3" requirement that seems to be employed by all Ws: blonde, black and busty. The clothes or the person can alternate between the first or second, the last one I'm convinced is a requirement.

The art of the order in many of these places is far more important than what is ordered. Nothing is a vodka tonic – no, it has to be Ketel One Vodka and tonic or maybe Grey Goose. It's a specificity that reflects a discernment and practice in making sure that every smallest detail in your existence is managed. That actual request is a brand sweet spot, the point where image advertising and celebrity sponsorships pay off in a 25 cent per pour premium.

"Tanqueray and tonic please," purrs Helen as she settles onto the lounge feeling sultry but slightly uncomfortable, because let's face it, mattresses are made for lying around on and it's hard to lie around when you are wearing US$400 Jimmy Choo's and a leather mini. It's even more agitating when you are in a bar filled with suits who are surprisingly discreet at checking out the said mini.

Eventually its time to repeat the scene at other places around town, and as the night gets later the music gets louder and the rooms take on an electronic neon luminescence. Air kiss dinner on the back porch at Park, whispers of who does what at the next table. Introductions that don't mean anything, but with cards filed away, *just in case*. Another rope. A back door. Into Lotus, and a quick nod past the bouncer into VIP, where the New York establishment sip on sake-tini's and roll an olive under the tongue. The models pout and flirt, the young bucks drink, and the music pumps.

Hate to quote the ancients, but like Madonna said, "music... makes the people... come together." This is especially true in the hubs, where HMV ensures that club kids in Hong Kong and Sydney are scooping up Jamiroquai at the same time he is making a radio debut across European airwaves, harmonizing a global moment that drives record sales. For most record companies hub sales account for the great majority of their global sales – without the hub tribes there would be no significant markets for international music that would justify the immediate release of the music in markets outside the artist's home. The role of music in leisure is strong, especially in the ability it has to unite the hubs in a common progressive beat and conversation.

The culture of hub nightlife and music developed over the last decade, growing principally from club culture that developed first in Europe and Australia's hubs, then found adaptation in hub cities around the world. It is not about an American export that is simply consumed by the other markets, even though it does include some American-produced content. It is about this culture actively seeking out a certain style of entertainment that draws from the influences of ethnic music, changing it from its original format and producing an evolution that can only be described as the Hub Aesthetic. Combined with the growth of nightlife in all the urban centers as a focal point for social interaction, the idea of a global groove has found a primary role in the culture. One would argue that music has long been global, but the point is that only recently have people actually experienced that music in the different hubs. This distinction has fostered a new globalism in music that has drawn it away from mass-produced pop culture run by the Americans.

Vanity Fair finally latched onto this idea in the fall of 2001 when it put Claude Challe and Stephane Pompangnovc on the Fanfair page of its annual music issue – a somewhat depressing moment for the hub identity given that these two had been poster children of the global group for about two years, and this action provided final, unmistakable proof, that this version of hub culture was about to move downstream, and out, to the mass markets. Through the turn of the millennium, there wasn't a dinner party where folks didn't simultaneously perk up and say, "Hey ... is this the new Buddha Bar?" which would invariably spark a 20-minute conversation on the new boys in town amid rampant disc flipping.

Since music by both artists were originally only sold at the Buddha Bar (Claude Challe's famous Asian-inspired Paris restaurant) or the Hôtel Costes (a baroque modern fantasy hotel where Stephane was the DJ, and his subsequent collections were branded), they were a little bit difficult to come by. Simply because they were scarce they had added cache, and the music became all the rage among the swifty set, with people dropping into both locations to buy the discs at a hefty premium. All that quickly ended in 2001 when the major record stores got wind of the duo and began selling the music in hub cities. Here the premium existed, but at a price point about 20% lower. Before you could snap your fingers, the wider craze was on for everyone who didn't have the wherewithal to drop by Paris. Fast forward another six months, and the whole collection was available in pirated version at many of the microhubs frequented by hub culture – beach and leisure destinations around the world, from Thailand to India to Latin America, for a fraction of the original price paid by the hub.

Music economics aside, Claude and Stephane get credit for popularizing a vibe that is very central to the core of this culture, and a combined sound that is here to stay. What *Vanity Fair* dubbed the "Parisian aesthetic" in its brief profile is actually just a segment of a much larger expressionism in music that is deliciously global in scope and influence. Its single biggest driving factor is that it takes everything around it – from J-pop to Spanish rhythms to country to gospel jazz, and imprints it with an interpretation that is distinct to this global culture, recognizable through its many forms.

It's like taking a local sound and processing it, in much the way cuisine has been processed. "Processing" implies a negative connotation, but this is not meant as a negative, it is simply the only way to describe this reinvention of the old into that new, evolved form of expression. In hub music, sometimes it's a beat, often it is an electronic overlay, but mostly it's an attitude that appreciates the roots of the music but is determined to reinvent the sound for a modern and non-rooted listening audience. The culture, remixed.

The other kings of the culture remixed must be the Café Del Mar Group and Hed Kandi, two series of dance and lounge compilations that took old music and added the new hub sound to the base, creating whole new markets for old classics from around the world. Because Café Del Mar grew from the early 1990s club culture found in Ibiza, and Hed Kandi grew from a more R&B, hip-hop base, they quickly found their own followings that soon crisscrossed, unifying the mix into a common sound that spans most of hub music. It is packaged, very packaged, but the hub likes the sound of that package and has bought it repeatedly.

The importance of the early- to mid- '90s Ibiza scene on global culture, and by extension Café del Mar, cannot be overstated – it is to the '90s what Woodstock was to the '60s, and was among the first places to distill the idea of a global groove.

Perhaps the remix vibe that grew from this scene has not been properly credited as a cultural statement with unique value because the changes it produces from the root are often interpreted as a statement against the original sound from which it originates. The creators of the sound are admittedly in it for the money, but that does not mean that they don't strive to create a sound that speaks to its audience, and is reflective of what their listening audiences demand.

It can also be said that this style of music and music production is a universal dub that has risen from club culture and Ecstasy, the most unifying, influential and far-reaching common entertainment base of the global hub. Ecstasy in particular has played a large role in creating a common experience among club-goers around the world. Drug use in general implies negative psychological and sociological side effects and Ecstasy may be no exception, but in the short term (during the user's experience), it undeniably provides a common base of understanding in large groups that has brought people together, with residual psychological effects. This in turn has created a common understanding that links the club generation globally. The same beats, the same dreamy smile, and the ability to say nothing and everything with a nod are elemental components of that experience.

The very fact that the Café Del Mar and Ministry of Sound empires grew from DJ collaborations verifies this idea of music and the culture remixed as being central to the hub experience. Now, the move of individual DJs to start their own projects outside of just clubs, such as Claude and Stephane's efforts with Buddha Bar and Costes in restaurants and hotels, shows the ongoing evolution in their work – a reflection of the maturing fan base and the changing tastes of the group. The ethnic vibe to the music grew because the DJs themselves spent so much time traveling – from Stockholm to Singapore to play parties at various clubs, they found an audience who wanted them to take their electronic-laced music into new areas: their own. The result was original work with Fahrsi, Indian and Latin influences that opened up a global audience to rooted music – provided that it was presented in the new expressionism grounded in electronic lace. Thus the Stockholm kids were psyched when they heard the latest sounds coming out of Tokyo and the rest of Asia, while the Tokyo kids lapped up the new work coming from London and Paris. Meanwhile DJ's from Tokyo and Beijing began to get gigs playing clubs across Europe, and everyone toured Miami, New York and LA, cementing the cross pollination of the scene.

Where do entertainers like Claude and Stephane get their vibe from? It is in the air around us. The music and nightlife industries have been the first to most completely feel this global hub identity. The beautiful young things that line up outside of New York's Bungalow 8, shiver outside Momo in London, and come rolling out of Hong Kong's Drop at dawn feel the same vibe because they are listening to the same music, and they keep hearing the same music in clubs that span Madrid to Sydney, Stockholm to Osaka. Granted, the prevailing vibe differs, like the fact that Beijing nightlife feels more like Nine Inch Nails compared to Sydney's Kylie Minogue, but the hub shifts with the vibe in each location as easily as it slips into and out of those different global cuisines.

The music is the same, even if the eye candy is not. It used to be that there was a good six to eight month lag before what was new in one location would catch on in others. Today, even though Ibiza is over, and travel is down, communication is better than ever. The club scene picks it up instantly, everywhere. No one even blinks about it anymore. It is no longer unusual that during the big East Indian thing, which was preceded by the cowboy look and rose-tinted glasses, (which coincided with turquoise mania) all of which was followed by '50's elegance, you ran virtually no risk of not knowing what was going on – it was in every hub at the same time, and ended everywhere within weeks of each other as the group moved onto the next thing.

The sound moves quickly, adopting the flavor of the moment with speed and accuracy that can only reflect the thinking of the audience it is designed to reach because it is only produced by the audience itself.

Post 9.11, the Middle Eastern trains and mullah wails of hub music quickly gave way to traditional Americana rock with a faint nu-metal thread, but in the same way that DJs updated and adapted music from other countries, the American roots of their new sound changed into something new, drawing from the origins of the music while interpreting it for the global culture.

Disposable culture that goes as quickly as it comes is a key facet of the hub experience and the result of a never-ending supply of content and products hurled at this audience. There is a lot of focus on new, even if it means simply remixing the old. In the case of music and other non-tangible cultural landmarks, this is fine; it keeps the scene interesting and provides room for many different contributions from a wide variety of sources. There is an egalitarian acceptance of the new that drives this constant turnover, and the departure of the last hot thing is not lamented anymore than the new hot thing is criticized for its arrival.

Every new sound is seen as an experience, a culturally enriching moment. As such, the only enduring thing becomes change, which the hub has learned to expect and embrace, even crave. The collective consciousness of the hub embraces the new, virtually simultaneously, only to leave it, virtually simultaneously.

Par example, it's Sunday night in Miami, and Mark is handing out flyers for a condo party to watch the Madonna tour on HBO. Nothing big, but these things are always a little bit of a production. Out go the printed flyers, bejeweled and featuring some blonde diva in a cowboy hat in a look that was pretty much disco cowboy. At the time it was cool and fresh, a new enough look for people to see it and think, "hot." Well, I thought it was groovy, and evocative of a common consciousness at the time which I couldn't quite put my finger on. I didn't know what until a few weeks later, when some random girl I met at a party handed me a bejeweled flyer announcing her birthday party… complete with a very similar girl chomping on some hay and sporting a similar hat… in Hong Kong. The point is not that they used the same stock pictures probably downloaded from the Internet (which is itself a cultural statement), but that hub people in Hong Kong and Miami both had a similar idea of what was cool for that moment, a common aesthetic defined by the home made invitation choices of two random, totally unconnected individuals as far separated as they could possibly be in a geographical sense. This was pre-Madonna's *Music*, her famous album that catapulted that "look" into the mainstream, where it was no longer surprising.

A Step Ahead

All that said, the sound in some hubs does tend to be a swing ahead of others, because even the best and most quickly adopted ideas have to originate from somewhere. They don't just magically appear. Although London and New York get kudos for being the most influential in this nightlife sense, other smaller hubs periodically play a role as arbiter and trend starter. Similar to Japan's fascination with consumer kitsch, Sydney makes a major contribution to the hub identity by the lifestyle and nightlife scenario it spins to the outside world.

Sydney has a certain swing to it that comes from being "discovered," a curious attribute that arises from being a major destination on the "it" list for quite some time. No location remains truly remote, but, let's face it, the sheer distance to the place from most of the major continents intoxicates the locals with a determined fatalism that says, "We can do whatever we want, and better," while providing the visitor with the sense that they truly are at the end of the earth, and therefore, it's fresh. There is in Sydney a healthy respect for livability (that fuzzy quality that encompasses clean drinking water and cockroach control) that eludes some other hub cities.

Sydney qualifies as a major hub because it actually has tremendous influence on the rest of the world, especially London, and it has the confidence to tell the rest of the world to fuck off when it doesn't like something. Perhaps the single largest factor contributing to Sydney's status as a hub city comes from club culture, which found a splendid home in Australia, centered from Sydney. Here, club culture and youth have created a tourism industry that goes far beyond traditional sites and locations like the Harbour Bridge and Sydney Opera House.

People come to Sydney to party, and to sample some of the best house music in the world at huge parties that span days. The growth of club culture in Sydney and the export of music and other cultural exports to the rest of the world have greatly contributed to the buzz and motivated people to get there. Of course the Olympics didn't hurt either, but for the hubs, club culture played a large role in putting this city within the intellectual reach of anybody with a OneWorld membership.

This is the Sydney package that the hub has created for itself, inventing a reality that serves the hub's vision of what Sydney should be: a collage of images that involve a laid-back, friendly attitude, a dead glo-stick and board shorts from the surf shop at the airport; the essential Sydney.

Part of the Sydney vision comes from its number-one export: the legions of Australians who, right now, are bartending or working in any number of hub cities, especially London and other big European cities. The great Australian walkabout, also popular with Kiwis, has cemented Australia's contribution to global culture. What better way to promote your country than to send all your best-looking kids abroad for a year to seed the cities of global commerce, where they absorb some form of best practices for global living, and evangelize to the great urban unconverted.

These same workers and travelers eventually return to Australia, and their experiences and ideas help to cultivate Sydney's global view.

Spirituality Through Sport

Subject: Fw: Tokyo Water Park
Date: Monday, Dec 03, 11:31:13 +20:00

Reply | Reply All | Forward | Delete | Previous | Next | Close

> **This is a picture of Tokyo Water Park where its slogan reads ...**
>
> **"Welcome to breathtaking Tokyo Water Park where you can wash away the pressure and stress of the overcrowded city and relax with your friends in the soothing enjoyment of sun, fun and splashing."**
>
> **Please see attached nice picture of nice Tokyo Water Park.**
>
> **Unfortunately, some of my friends from Tokyo may not understand the humor in this.**
>
> **(next page water–park image)**

The image contained an aerial snapshot of about 3,000 people bathing in a large public pool outside of Tokyo. Here, we are faced with the harsh reality that not everything in local culture is transferable to hub culture. The idea of communal enjoyment that so entails a visit to a waterpark with 3,000 others just doesn't register with the hub culture, Asian or not. Leisure is more personal than that.

What does register is the idea of using leisure, especially sport, to achieve a sense of mental and spiritual clarity that is a refuge from the pressures of material existence. As such, sport is becoming part of the new spirituality, a path to connection with the higher, non-material self. In so doing, the expectation about what sport and its role in leisure should offer us is changing dramatically, leaving a door wide open to reach the hub culture above the material level. Sport is an opportunity to catch them on their journey to transform the physical into the spiritual.

<Vienna, Saturday morning>
Lea and her boyfriend have just pumped through another weight training class, but they are about to bail on their gym membership because they are sick of the very idea of the gym.

Gym culture is starting to wane for the hub culture just as it becomes a must-do attitude for downstream markets. Gold's Gym, California Fitness, the body mecca Crunch, are all running out of steam. Now if you can get 20 people into a spin class the instructor is delighted, even though they are the same classes that were packed with waiting lists only three years ago. After steadily rising in membership across urban areas throughout the '90s and into the new decade, the growth has reversed in the hubs – resulting in fewer flat stomachs and a new, more casual acceptance of girth. To be fair, a two-sided dilemma has always plagued the US, where the population generally erred on the side of super fit or super fat, with little psychological room left in between. As the economy mellowed so have the ambitions to be perfect – and the result is a body consciousness that is shifting away from the rock-hard physiques and toward a softer, but still healthy, body shape. In other words, now it's all about yoga.

But there is something deeper in this move away from pumping iron and treadmill addiction.

The shift away from the '90s ideal is a result of more than the typical excuses – that people don't have time, that "if J-Lo packs back so can I," etc. It's vitally important to be at the cutting edge in urban life, and the fact is that gym life has become stale, like much of the rest of the social theme to "just do it" that it embodies.

It's more than the fact that people have huffed and puffed their way through gyms and dance clubs (in different forms) for the last 10 years. The ubiquity of gym culture and club culture, complete with the same music in different settings, means that people are starting to simply feel ambivalent about the whole concept. It has become as material as shopping. There is fatigue not for fitness and feeling good but for the way it is delivered. In an era where the most valuable commodity is time and the constant demand is for a link to your spiritual self, or at the very least entertainment, fitness must conform or risk irrelevance.

Gyms are fighting back in an effort to retain people and offer something new – but what's on the horizon will change the way we view exercise and socialization as a part of fitness. The first response has been to start making fitness entertaining. In Tokyo and Hong Kong, even Singapore, the Western gym concept of watching television while you run, earphones plugged in, is starting to go a step further toward a more complete virtual entertainment experience. As the multi-player Internet phenom and persistent universe gaming start to take off with consumers, the ideal format for large, multi-user applications becomes today's humble gym. Persistent universe gaming is already a major force in the lives of many teenagers – video games that continue to evolve or change whether the user is online and participating or not. If the user leaves the game, she may come back to find the setting and the world of the game altered, changed by other users who have interacted in the universe during her absence.

Soon, this will be applied to gyms, creating an entirely new physical entertainment industry. Wired, gyms will become a workout location that enables members to compete against each other in elaborate online settings. It is even likely that the online identity of the user will be a construct, a virtual skin. At the very least, this far exceeds running the pollution-choked streets of the typical urban metropolis with your neighbor as a running partner. At the most, it takes the mental monotony out of the treadmill. That covers the entertainment part.

But the bigger trend is for a holistic spiritual application of fitness. Hence the yoga. Increasing numbers of hub people have modified their motivation for working out toward that search for spirituality. Exercise becomes less about looking good or for health reasons, and more about connecting their mind, their body and their spirit in one blank savasana slate. This goes farther than the purely physical benefits of a good workout, which many gym addicts will tell you is a primary motivator. But real spirituality, trying to reach God, so to speak, is at the center of the booming demand for yoga, Pilates, even kickboxing to be presented in a way that will better you as a person in the rest of your life, long after the effects of a good workout have left your body. It is about finding an existence that is more focused, more balanced, more in tune with the connections that move you.

The Third Space in London is an example of the first wave of holistic gyms coming onto the market. It is very well named. Created as a space between home and work, for living and self development, it is true to the ideals of hub culture. It is proudly as much a spiritual club as it is a gym, offering a variety of services and options that delve more into lifestyle management, with fitness the focus of the core offering. Here, members enjoy the standard benefits of a gym with classes that focus on everything from nutrition to stress management. Gospel Aerobics allows you to worship while you sweat. Live DJs spin the latest sounds, and the yoga classes are packed, with many different forms of meditation and exercise-based regimes available to suit individual tastes. There is a lounge, an organic food center, a deli and juice-bar, and massage and relaxation offerings. This is the gym of the future, one that mixes holistic well-being for the mind, body and soul with exercise in an attempt to deliver the spiritual nirvana that the hub seeks.

But just because it strives to connect with these higher ideals does not mean that there will not be a place for products of similar theosophical background in the new space. Tremendous opportunity for marketers will exist in the realm of product placement and image enhancement through these gym concepts. Imagine a spin class that embodies the traditional fast beats and belted music track with a class that pedals facing a giant moving screen or a series of personal TVs tuned to the performance of each bike, similar to the way today's road racing games enable multi-user formats. A roadway, a trail, a course; they all will change over the course of the class. Product placement and virtual usage opportunities will exist for companies along this route – from the Volvo that passes in front you to the Niketown at the corner, to the FedEx drop-off box on the side of the road. With a wired bike and personal gym account based on the web, you will be able to track your own workout history and performance variables online, charting progress and development while building a case history. For the gym, it will be possible to create an automated function that runs largely at the user's discretion, and the result – increased loyalty, will be a great benefit worth the investment in technology to keep consumers coming back. The debut of these types of services will also lead to interesting ethical choices about privacy – will this heart rate and athletic performance data be available to your insurance company or the marketers who try to sell products that will enhance your performance? If you are a marketer, how do you ingratiate yourself to the end-users, your customers, to perfectly pitch your product to their needs and aspirations?

The framework for this sort of user experience and the questions it creates for marketers are coming from current video and gaming technology, already available in some format both in Microsoft's Xbox and Sony's Sega series. When this technology starts to find application in presently offline categories, such as the gym industry, expect major transformative growth.

When there's time, hub culture tries to mix leisure with pursuits outside gym through extreme, or at least unusual, sports. If that can be combined with travel, so much the better, and hence the fascination with micro-hubs, the niche locations that offer the social interactivity that comes with the adventure break.

The conversations that pervade these locations are eerily similar, whether you are abseiling from the edge of Table Mountain, paragliding outside of Taipei, or heli-skiing in the Himalayas. Central to all of them is hub psychology – a few ideas about life and leisure that are constant.

[1] Sport through nature is a path to spirituality.

[2] The experience of non-repeated leisure is of great importance – i.e. you master a skill and move on.

[3] Technology will solve our problems – especially physical, by the time we are old enough to worry about it.

The grin on Hakan's face is almost convincing. "So there are four of us going, two of my friends from London and one from Turkey. You should come. It's going to be such a rush. We can do five because the choppers only take three at a time on the runs."

Hakan is on the home stretch of six months planning for a heli-skiing tour of the back Himalayas. Eighteen peaks in six days, with nothing but a guide, a pilot and simple provisions for hut stays at rural mountain bases. The net cost is not much more than a week at a nice resort in the Caribbean, but for him far more enticing. This is the latest in a series of adrenaline rushes – sailing in the Maldives, mountain climbing in Africa and the burning desire to make it farther than Everest base camp. All of it is a quest to connect with something larger than himself, while using proximity to this spirituality as a route to something "pure."

"You feel so close to yourself – it's such a challenge, and you're skiing down powder no one has even seen, let alone skied. It's not like it is that dangerous, but it's going to be a thrill. This will definitely top anything I've done before."

Hakan, like many hub culture people, wants to be as successful a part-time adventure boy as he is a full-time business deal maker. Interestingly, his stories of extreme leisure also fill the gap in business dinner conversations, helping him develop his overall personal brand, reputation and trust levels with clients.

A similar picture develops when we go back to Scott, the Colorado guy who found his professional and travel life mixing to create a hybrid personality, which he tried to juggle at home and away. In turn, his leisure choices reinforce that mix, and he puts a focus on this extreme leisure to find a spiritual connection to himself. This time it is with climbing, and the consequences of pushing himself to his physical limits.

Scott rhapsodizes as he puts down his drink. "We call it 'doing the Elvis.' And don't worry, it happens to everybody, no matter how much you practice or how strong you are. You just learn to control it. Girls actually have an advantage, they're used to pushing with their legs more, whereas guys tend to pull with their arms. You want to keep your arms straight, so you don't tire yourself out, but when you find yourself horizontal and your feet are barely planted on the edge and your arms are spread about 10 feet, it will start. Doesn't matter who you are ...

"I did some bouldering today and we'll do a rope climb on Monday. Tomorrow's a rest day, so we're going to take the kayaks over to the far side and check out a couple climbs there."

The conversation rambles in the night air, and soon the bartender and his friends slide around the small wooden semicircle, quietly asking if anyone wants a last drink. Then the generator cuts out and the dozen or so left sitting around the long wooden plank drift into darkness, faintly outlined by the pink silhouette of a lone disco light. Thailand.

Meanwhile, somewhere in the Himalayas, Hakan is drinking hot tea in the snow by a fire, talking with a group of travelers he doesn't know but feels connected to, because they are of the same mind.

Scott changes the subject, introducing a topic that is discussed all over hub culture at various points and times. "I can't wait to get new body parts. I really need new shoulders. I've ruined them climbing."

Brows furrow.

The beer is still only half empty, and as he takes another little sip, he answers the inevitable questions that follow such a statement, mediated by adjoining stories and examples. The news of prosthesis that can outperform natural limbs floats out, along with a collective wish for eternal youth. "I wonder when they'll be able to farm body parts, so you can just grow another replacement. I'll get everything changed as I need it."

There is some agreement as the others think about the idea of never growing old, of simply replacing themselves if only to prolong the quality of themselves. In this group, it's not about age, it's about the quality of the age, and the moral dilemmas don't apply. It is as if our generation has already internalized and rationalized everything to do with maintenance, self improvement and living longer; deciding that no consequence of technology is really so terrible as to consider not moving forward with the research and experimentation it requires. Without it, we risk missing out.

So cloning organs holds little in the way of moral discomfort. It is complemented by a certain naivete peculiar to the hub: that despite all the cynicism, we all want to believe what popular culture tells us. In this instance, it is that science is close to solving our problems and our diseases, the curse of age, arthritis and cancer and torn ligaments ... which means that we can go hell for leather now and it will all be cleaned up and fixable later. Ah, denial.

"There is always a moral dilemma with technology, but it sorts itself out in the end. Like I'm sure when they invented the wheel they never knew people would die in car accidents, but I think we'd all agree we're better off for it." Scott's analogy is a bit rough, but his point remains: he thinks it will all be OK. Not only does he think it will all be OK, he fully expects that he will be able to replace whatever is worn out and in need of replacement with items that could actually improve his performance; fulfilling the bionic dream of a '70s-born generation that grew up watching the "Six Million Dollar Man" and superheroes with androidian features.

For hub culture, the reference points are science, technology and the glow of inner health that pervade the new global consumer culture – largely driven by media representation of a bright and beautiful future where all our wildest dreams will come true. It's holistic.

This is naïve, but it does sell.

As Scott downs the last of his beer and Hakan dumps himself on the downhill powder, doors are opening half way around the world for another day of business at a company called Biomet Inc. based in Warsaw, Indiana, a decidedly non-hub location. The small biotech company specializes in joint and fixture replacement and is exactly the kind of company we picture when we think of those advanced, clinical biotech firms that are going to change the world. The company does about US$70 million in reconstructed shoulders annually, so they are fairly knowledgeable about how likely Scott's vision of a replaceable body (or hey, even just a shoulder) really is.

"It's not. Unfortunately," says Charles Niemier, Biomet's senior vice president of international operations.

Niemier says that the point where prosthetics and replacements actually match human performance is still a long way off, and may not ever be possible, simply because the technology, in its current form, has significant limitations that will not be surmounted before bio-engineering replaces it.

Other companies such as Biogen, a leading biotechnology firm that has operations in Germany, the US and Japan, among other places, are banking on this very fact, but even it doesn't see full replacements happening any time soon. In fact, the elimination of a host of other problems that hub culture expect to see within our lifetime – from cancer through to genetic manipulation of DNA code to prevent disease, is farther away than the hub think.

Another aspect of leisure-related denial comes in the hub's approach to, and adoration of, their toys. The toys vary. In extreme sports it is about the best ski equipment and thousands of dollars of harnesses and other items for the proper climbing experience. In regular life, it is about the gadgets – communicators and BlackBerrys and phones, or the right accessories for car culture.

Scott likes his toys. "I think it's worse than a drug habit. Certainly more expensive. It's the same rush you know, you've got to get more and more, the best stuff. Take climbing: you've got to have the right shoes, that's $200. Chalk. Harness. Ropes aren't cheap. Going to and from places where I can find a good climb. You just spend a fortune.

"It's addictive, material life. Because I have so many necessities. If it's not climbing, it's something else. And I always have to have the right gear, because, like I said, I like my toys."

He hasn't even mentioned what he drives, but the look on his face indicates that this, the most important of "the toys," mirrors an even greater attention to detail, and spending.

Travel, toys and the pursuit of "the perfect life." It's a constant drive that crosses all aspects of hub culture, from work to leisure, even relationships. People are driven by common links and a growing network of experience that is decidedly post-national. The hub culture employs more than a whiff of disdain for traditional advertising and marketing while simultaneously cherry-picking materialism. The group relies on word of mouth to determine what's hot, fully aware that word of mouth is greatly influenced by the mass media and marketing. Above all this is the idea that quality of life is the Holy Grail, influenced by an ephemeral global aesthetic.

This is now: Fast start. Hard stop. High-octane living punctuated by periods of self-imposed exile. Ambivalence that alternates with angst that you're missing out. On something. Somewhere. No matter where you are. Refined taste. Elevated subculture. But still itchy. One hundred e-mails a day. One thousand things to do. A weekend away, waitlisted to four different destinations. Thinking about your next city. But not sure which one. A total disregard for passport control. And finally, the realization that with all that to think about, you can't remember yesterday. Or worse yet, anything about it. Thus, you have to continuously look forward, or focus on today. Right now becomes the next big thing. It's Zen on crack.

Hakan: "What did I do last summer? So long ago. Not sure. I think it was fun."

As a marketer trying to reach hub people through their association with leisure, it is important to realize that your group can't love you, or be loyal to you, if they can't remember you. And they will forget you quickly. The cheapest way to get them to remember you is to stick with them by developing a personal relationship that is less about consumption, and more about linking to their spiritual quest, which they never forget. You've got to get the brand above the fray, in sync with their ideals. Leisure is one of the few environments in which that can be done.

chapter**twelve**
Popsicle Backlash

"I would rather take the green paper that the stick people give to me and hang it on a wall than take it and better my own life because that's how brainwashed I am." – *toilet stall graffiti, Flagstaff, Arizona*

Even rebellious, disenfranchised protesters now understand that ideology has become as packaged as anything else they come into contact with. What is not commonly noted is that the people of hub culture, consumed by their own consumption, to which the protest movement imagines it is fundamentally opposed, is subject to the same disillusionment. The hub's imagined antithesis, the anti-globalization, anti-consumer rebel, is in fact little different from them. Passive, ambivalent backlash exists within the hub to such a great extent that it is accepted with the same shrug of the shoulders that greets everything else.

Meanwhile, the loudest critics of the current order, those who lead it, are as ignorantly opposed to those who swell the bottoms of their own ranks as they are the corporations they fight. Because down at the bottom, the protester has come to the same conclusion as the hub: the "revolution" against branding as an oppressive, unavoidable force has already been packaged and sold to us, perhaps accidentally, but sold none the less. Why is it that the people "in charge" are always last to figure things like that out?

As the opening quote demonstrates, even those outside the hubs have come to the realization that Greenpeace angst is not much different from 'N Sync idolatry, which again is no different from the Falun Gong. It's just a matter of finding your own personal crusade. The angst and disillusionment that come with materialism and what brands now offer the consumer are pervasive, in all markets. It's not news to anyone.

Erin, 21, labor activist, Mexico City: "Angst is over. We're all eating from the same Popsicle. You just choose the flavor, that's all."

Even the movements that are trying to fight the global consumer culture have become as caught up in the presentation of their cause as the very institutions they were established to confront. People forget that the International Monetary Fund and World Bank started as weak, fringe organizations. They were rebellious to the nationalistic order of then dominant institutions and have, over time, moved from the outside of majority thought and perception to the center. Originally they espoused a rebel quality against the order of their era. Now they are seen as the core of the existing establishment.

In the same way, previously disenfranchised movements such as Committee for Global Justice, protest.net and Greenpeace are now more global than some multinationals they protest against, and they are run in the same way that the companies themselves are run.

This is good for the long-term survival of these organizations – they adapt and fit into an ever-changing world and try to influence the issues that they want to address from a more moderate tone of conversation – more successful than the anti-globalization groups that ran into such problems at the G7 meetings in Canada, Genoa and the Battle of Seattle in 1999. But, eventually, these groups will be co-opted into the establishment as well, to be challenged by a new radicalism down the road.

But no matter how "establishment" or how "fringe" these revolt organizations become, none of their thinking makes them very different from their imagined antithesis, a pepsi.com-based Britney Spears Spanish fan club.

Everybody has an agenda, some more benign than others, but it really is all about individuals choosing their Popsicle flavor – it could be Scandinavian radical environmentalism, Berlin neo-punk rock groupie, India ashram yoga vegan, Sydney gym jock or Tokyo corporate day-trader, or most likely, any combination of those categories depending on the day. Most people in hub culture seem to have come to this same realization, an enlightenment that has bred bored tolerance to nearly everything, with very little internal association to their real identity. With the speed at which hub culture consumes and disposes of trends and goods, the ability to select these identities off the rack allows us to be like the culture itself: everything, and again, nothing.

The reasons why real revolution doesn't last in the hub culture are closely tied to the efficiency in which the never-ending cycle of disposability adopts the subculture and deifies it for the hub to consume. When the hub demands "revolution" they get it, even if that means it must be packaged in the *Matrix* and *American Beauty*, *nologo.org*, the *Lonely Planet Pocket Guide to Bangladesh* and *battleshields for Alberta*.

The culture recycles everything subversive that it touches, sort of like some sort of super-goop disinfectant. Much of this comes from the style-trackers and the corporate individuals who come into contact with the subculture on a regular basis in an attempt to identify with the latest mood of the hub, whom both sides represent equally.

The backlash becomes more sterile the more radical it becomes, because at any end of the spectrum the circles and networks become as important, global and obvious as they are at any point in the most branded portion of the elite hub culture. It's almost like radicalism and anti-brand fervor have become an ironic inside joke that everybody gets: global corporations "fear" the revolt of the non-hub masses against their products and respond by producing products that appeal to their angst. Meanwhile, hub creatures blithely consume brands with mock loyalty, aware of the emptiness it provides, but sated with the proxy for spirituality that it is. Regardless, their loyalty is gone with the next product cycle, or as soon as they forget it.

The irony of the revolution extends back to the individual, where even personal claimants to the branding backlash or those who claim spiritual enlightenment employ a sardonic acceptance of the commercial.

The guy behind the cult-kitsch website www.jesus.com is the joke that is modern irony. His website (probably accidentally) personifies the anti-hub by extremes, to such an extent that he actually exhibits a very similar view as the people of hub culture itself. He is so far around the bend he's back again. But he is a reflection of the broader identity: amid a never-ending adoption, evolution and disposal by ourselves, down to the individual level, of the new culture, we create it by and for ourselves. Hub culture is its own food.

A mix of personal ad, sermons that involve everything from pagan Easters to Kurt Cobain's death, plus a restaurant guide for good measure, www.jesus.com is a true example of the cynicism people have about the mix of spirituality with branding and materialism that permeates their lives.

Jesus, as he calls himself, happily talks about his rejection of the material world and his quest for spiritual satisfaction and enlightenment, while prostituting his spiritualization to organize joint bathing opportunities with equally cynical young women. At the end of the day, it is simply an extremely elaborate attempt to market himself for a long-term relationship. Jesus cheerfully absorbs what pop icons seem appropriate to him personally and mushes them together to create his own personal statement, the ultimate result of a culture that absorbs, evolves and disposes of whatever it comes into contact with.

As such, he has taken his quest for spirituality and put it right back to where he started, in the model of consumption. He is thus no farther in his development and his form of protest, of backlash, is effectively sterilized. He has only flipped his coin.

The real backlash, the dangerous backlash, (evident in isolated pockets) rejects materialism in its entirety without the comfort of spirituality. This leaves nothing to connect your identity with, for you forsake the proxy, but do not gain the real thing. You thus end up not on one side or the other of the same coin, but off it.

<Washington, D.C., Friday afternoon>
Downtown, amid the slow hustle of a city that is, in its heart, southern, a different world co-exists with the beautiful creatures that inhabit the air-kiss lands of MCCXXIII and Café Milano in Georgetown. The sheen that is America's prosperity has glossed over the rocketing class differences that increasingly separate Americans from themselves. When your community is gated and your work day is 12 hours, punctuated only by dinner in Adam's Morgan and cocktails in Cleveland Park, it is easy to forget that affluence, everywhere, is taken for granted.

A stop into a downtown Burger King highlights a striking parallel universe, a shadow off the coin. In this case it is the restaurant as a community center. Similar to the quaint, faintly sexy notion of 20-somethings hanging out at Starbucks with their notebook computers working on consulting gigs (the mobile professional, freed from cubicle-land) this location attracts the afternoon unemployed and serves as a babysitting location for a working mom, stuck in the ultimate McJob. She desperately hopes that no customers bitch her out for the two kids playing hide and seek under the tables, under strict orders to be as well mannered as possible.

The shadow is in social welfare, where Hong Kong professionals side step beggars on the street, blind to their existence. The shadow is in the corners of the megalopolis, where millions of people observe, but do not partake of, the fruits of materialism. And the shadow is within ourselves, for when the culture eventually disposes of its very core, its people, an echo develops when you realize that your value to others is defined by how much you can consume. It is at that point, if you haven't somehow connected to something larger, past the material existence, that you find hate and despair. For nothing lasts, and since consumption, by its very core, is temporary, it happens to everyone sooner or later.

Jesus sums it up by pulling another hub story from the shadows, processing it and turning it into a product for consumption of others. But in this particular story is a lesson of what happens when you wake up to the material side's emptiness, but fail to connect with the spiritual plane above it.

Even though Kurt Cobain's suicide was over ten years ago, it remains a timeless lesson that transcends the confines of Cobain as an individual. The rise of his band, Nirvana, and his subsequent death marked the start of "angst" in pop culture and was one of the first pockets of backlash seen to bubble to the surface of the American landscape. The generation that came of age around that time subsequently became the "voice" of much of the cultural expression found in hub culture today, and that dissatisfaction and restlessness has moved and grown with the group. Cobain connected with his audience in a strange and real way, and the frustration that consumed him is felt by many still today. His was a pocket of sad personal rebellion, but the underlying message he sent has the potential to connect to other pockets of disillusionment and protest in broader culture.

<Kurt Cobain's suicide note, from Jesus.com>
To Boddah:

Speaking from the tongue of an experienced simpleton who obviously would rather be an emasculated, infantile complain-ee. This note should be pretty easy to understand.

All the warnings from the punk rock 101 courses over the years, since my first introduction to the, shall we say, ethics involved with independence and the embracement of your community had proven to be very true. I haven't felt the excitement of listening to as well as creating music along with reading and writing for too many years now. I feel guilty beyond words about these things.

For example, when we're backstage and the lights go out and the manic roar of the crowds begins, it doesn't affect me the way in which it did for Freddie Mercury, who seemed to love, relish in the love and adoration from the crowd which is something I totally admire and envy. The fact is, I can't fool you, any one of you. It simply isn't fair to you or me. The worst crime I can think of would be to rip people off by faking it and pretending as if I'm having 100% fun.

Sometimes I feel as if I should have a punch-in time clock before I walk out on stage. I've tried everything within my power to appreciate it (and I do, God, believe me I do, but it's not enough). I appreciate the fact that I and we have affected and entertained a lot of people. I must be one of those narcissists who only appreciate things when they're gone. I'm too sensitive.

I need to be slightly numb in order to regain the enthusiasms I once had as a child.

On our last 3 tours, I've had a much better appreciation for all the people I've known personally, and as fans of our music, but I still can't get over the frustration, the guilt and empathy I have for everyone. There's good in all of us and I think I simply love people too much, so much that it makes me feel too fucking sad. The sad little, sensitive, unappreciative, Pisces, Jesus man. Why don't you just enjoy it? I don't know!

I have a goddess of a wife who sweats ambition and empathy and a daughter who reminds me too much of what I used to be, full of love and joy, kissing every person she meets because everyone is good and will do her no harm. And that terrifies me to the point to where I can barely function. I can't stand the thought of Frances becoming the miserable, self-destructive, death rocker that I've become.

I have it good, very good, and I'm grateful, but since the age of seven, I've become hateful towards all humans in general. Only because it seems so easy for people to get along that have empathy. Only because I love and feel sorry for people too much, I guess.

Thank you all from the pit of my burning, nauseous stomach for your letters and concern during the past years. I'm too much of an erratic, moody baby!

I don't have the passion anymore, and so remember, it's better to burn out than to fade away.

Peace, love, empathy,
Kurt Cobain

Frances and Courtney, I'll be at your altar.
Please keep going Courtney, for Frances.
For her life, which will be so much happier without me.

I love you, I love you!

In this instance, backlash reaches conclusion at the following decision: the only way to save ourselves is to destroy ourselves. As long as we exist, the fight between having and not having, of finding and losing, will exist. Part of the reason Cobain connected so well with people was that he was among the first to realize what many people now see. Because consumption in hub culture is only a reflection of our demand, it reflects what we see as important and dismisses what we don't see as important. If the product or the company is no longer useful, you lose it. If the person is no longer relevant, you dismiss it. That is harder on people than it is on companies and products. The roar dies, and the wave rolls back (whatever it is) and you either have something or you don't.

Either way, as an individual brand or as a marketer trying to build and sell a brand, you have to get yourself past that level, because eventually, no matter how popular the person or the product, it becomes clear that there has to be something more, something that drives us to create and produce and live.

If the link is to find a spiritual connection that bolts you past the mere proposition of selling yourself, your services, or your products in a pure supply-and-demand way then you have to get onto a spiritual plane, tied to our deeper existence. Then you save yourself.

This spiritual plane is where many people in hub culture are trying to get to now, and smart brands and marketers are trying to get there too, so they can hold them when the quest for material status, or that roar of the crowd, fades.

For others who understand and choose to reject the hollow mirage of materialism, but do not find that spiritual peace, the second alternative, the Cobain way, may seem like a viable alternative. That is the ultimate backlash, and it's even more poignant when it's about forcing others to the same conclusion.

So it may be there are two stages with an option: drink the Kool-Aid of materialism and forget, or wake up and see it for what it is. Seek spiritual understanding, or go Columbine.

For brands and marketing and selling, the value proposition, the ideal you want to be close to, is the spiritual. Blind consumption is done. The latter is obviously a future no one wants.

chapter thirteen

How to Build a Phenomenon on a Shoestring

Subject: branding, the short version
Date: Sunday, June 9, 2002 11:24:00 +0800

Reply | Reply All | Forward | Delete | Previous | Next | Close

You go to a party and you see an attractive female across the room. You walk up to her and say, "Hi, I'm great in bed."

This is an example of direct marketing.

You go to a party and you see an attractive female across the room. You give your mate $10 to approach her and say "Hi, my friend over there (pointing to you) is great in bed."

This is an example of advertising.

You go to a party and you see an attractive female across the room. You get two of your female friends to stand within earshot of her and talk about how great you are in bed.

This is an example of PR.

> **You go to a party and you see an attractive female across the room. She immediately walks over and says, "Hi, I hear you're great in bed."**
>
> **This is an example of branding.**

The above observation, which has been floating around the Internet and by e-mail, is a good (if crass) example of the components that make up the branding equation, whether you are targeting hub culture or not. To be successful, you need to master these tools and use them with planned surgical precision.

In the context of this example, we all want to be "great in bed" when it comes to how others see our business and the products we offer to the market. But getting there requires a few fundamentals: a great product, good service and enough experience with the right people to make sure that word of mouth travels.

The right people are in the hubs and word of mouth remains the most important aspect of developing brand awareness with the group. But to build word of mouth, you really need to use the direct marketing, advertising and PR tools to create the final "it moment," that moment when someone new walks up to you and says she wants it, whatever it is, before you have to make the effort to go and convince her she wants it. The quickest way to set word of mouth in motion is to target your direct marketing, advertising and PR to the people who make up hub culture, letting them use their influence, connectivity and mobility to spread the message for you.

To create that positive brand awareness and personal connection that spur them to act in favor of your product, it helps to tie your identity to those aspects that are important to the lives of the people in hub culture – basing your message around that global consciousness to which they aspire and to which they can relate. Focus on the core traits, linking your message to them through travel, virtual communication, relationships and networks, the goal of professional advancement, or a desire for leisure, and remember to manage the negative side of the new global culture and its attendant backlash so tightly woven into the new consumption psyche by subtly addressing social concerns and the relationship between the spiritual-material conflict.

Let's start with direct marketing. No matter the size of the company, direct marketing starts with a solid strategy to develop lasting customer relationships. It is the foundation of building sales and the one opportunity you as a producer have to speak directly with your potential clients. It is where the majority of a marketing focus should be spent and should account for the largest portion of a marketing and brand-building budget. The rise of personal communication and the Internet have engendered great advances in the development and maintenance of these customer relationships, allowing even large companies to foster deeper individual discussions with the clients who purchase from them, both on the consumer and the business-to-business side.

There is a golden rule in business that 20% of your customers account for 80% of your sales, and it is to this 20% that the bulk of a customer relationship management strategy should be weighted. Customer relationship management, CRM, has been the hot topic for several years now and is really so wide that it can include everything from an e-mail blast announcing a promotion to data mining for color preferences to taking a big client out for dinner or a game of golf.

The important thing to remember is that this direct communication is the most important part of developing loyal relationships.

In 2001, FORTUNE magazine released a summary brochure of the results of a co-sponsored research project between Trilogy and FORTUNE on customer relations. The study polled 429 top-level officers of the 1,000 largest companies in the US, asking them about their impressions of customer relations within FORTUNE 500 companies as well as within their own companies.

This research also examined their company's current CRM strategies both online and offline. Toward the end of the survey, senior executives were asked to vote on which FORTUNE 500 companies are best at managing customer relations from several standpoints including business-to-business and business-to-consumer customer relations.

The research showed that CRM and direct marketing are core elements in the success of their overall business strategies. Many of them said that customer service was the most important aspect of managing their customer relationships and that this direct contact had the biggest influence on their ability to build direct marketing relationships.

Within customer service, a quick response time to customer requests was deemed the most important factor, but less than 1% of those surveyed rated customer relations among FORTUNE 500 companies as "excellent." However, it is clearly important to the companies involved, as a majority (81%) gave them "very good" or "good" ratings and 85% of senior executives in those companies said that customer relations were "very" important to their company's core strategy, especially in a tight economy.

Among the FORTUNE 1000 it became evident that all companies have a long way to go in improving their CRM initiatives. Less than 10% found their own company "excellent" at customer relations, and only two-thirds have developed an online CRM strategy, perhaps the most influential factor in easing the task of personalized communication programs.

A digital strategy of service provision and communication has advantages in that it can filter easily-answered, time-wasting questions by posting information for easy consumption. Providing services such as general company information, online account tracking, or online service centers to handle basic requests frees up human resources to focus on unique, pressing problems that require a more personal interaction model. If your staff is busy handling routine requests, they never gain the time to focus on real individual service with the 20% of those clients who need a deep, personal relationship. They also miss the opportunity to take steps to deepen the relationship that exists with other smaller clients who could account for a larger portion of the company's sales formula.

Some winners did come out of the survey, and they all employed a similar strategy: selling on price but delivering service. The FORTUNE 500 companies voted on who manages their customer relations the best, with Dell Computer and Southwest Airlines coming out on top. Both have invested greatly in the online portion of their customer service strategies, putting as much information as possible at the fingertips of their consumers while working to build a corporate culture that swiftly addresses client and consumer concerns. Best overall at managing B2B customer relations was Cisco Systems. Best at developing customer loyalty was Wal-Mart Stores.

One thing all of these companies have in common is an outward price-centric strategy supported by an internal focus on service – the main determinant of value in price preservation. Though they all outwardly sell on price, their real focus is on delivering good service as well, quietly exceeding the expectations of their customers by delivering more than just the product.

Good CRM is Simple, Great CRM is Expensive

Since speed is seen as critical to good CRM, simple solutions can have the greatest impact on the organization. It could even be as easy as compiling a list of the company's 10 biggest clients and making sure that everybody in the company knows who those clients are and how much they contribute to the company's overall revenue. Though it seems basic, most employees, especially in larger companies, don't know the answer to this question, and when they don't know, they don't care, and opportunities get missed. This applies all the way down to receptionists who take a call. Everyone has to know who is important and who is less critical, so that the entire organization can prioritize its actions – there are always more things to do than you have time for, and focusing the priorities where the money is will maximize long-term revenue for the company and build the best relationships where they are most needed.

Common access to internal information can also be very useful in jelling a sense of mission among employees, helping to more clearly determine the direction in which the next level of direct marketing communications (to the other 80%) should be moving. This access allows a company to anticipate changes in the client and customer base more effectively, because they can forecast trends over time, enabling them to tell which clients hold the greatest potential future return.

Costs of more elaborate CRM initiatives can quickly add up, especially when you are trying to make a patchwork of different databases and computer systems work together seamlessly. As a result, compatibility among data systems is of paramount importance and should be implemented in scaled architecture systems as early as possible.

The problem for many companies is that they tend to build their database and intelligence systems over older ones, making it difficult to scale or cross-reference the data down the road. In these cases it may be worth migrating as much data as possible to an open system – redeveloping the data in a new core and leaving the old systems as periphery units. This can be expensive, and it's why companies like Oracle and EDS make so much money.

Once you have worked out those issues, it's time to think about how to develop your direct marketing message. There are ways to do it without spending a fortune for little reply. Most direct mail response rates are estimated at 0.5-2% of the total mail-out, a pitiful return. So for every 10,000 pieces you send out, you can expect between only five to twenty replies.

And that's not even sales. Fortunately the number improves with a more personalized message, and in the case of the most intimate direct mail, a personal invitation, can reach as high as a 40% response rate. But that's the most you'll ever get.

Estimates from a Stuart Elliott story in the *New York Times* (October 16, 2001) show that in the US the direct-marketing industry sold about $528 billion worth of goods and services through the mail, but response from consumers is so low that wastage is a huge problem.

"The hardest thing we have to do as direct marketers is getting someone to open the envelope," said Howard Draft, chairman and chief executive at Draft Worldwide in Chicago, the largest direct marketing agency.

The article focused on a difficult way of selling that is only getting more difficult in the wake of increased consumer vigilance following the anthrax incidents.

"The difficulties generated by the anxieties over mystery mail are likely to make a challenging period even tougher for the industry, which was already grappling with an economic slowdown at its most important time of the year, the start of the holiday shopping season.

"The last time I talked to the mail people, they told me Sept. 11 had really cut into their response rates, particularly for credit-card solicitations and magazine subscription renewals," said Robert J. Coen, the longtime predictor of advertising spending, who is senior vice-president and forecasting director at Universal McCann in New York, part of the McCann-Erickson WorldGroup division of Interpublic.

"And this may carry over..." he added, "a lot of marketers are going to be worried." Mr. Coen had estimated that marketers would spend $46.6 billion on advertising mail this year, compared with $44.6 billion in 2000."

The great expense compared to a small return, plus the huge wastage associated with the direct-mail industry stem from the fact that a message just doesn't feel personal when it arrives in your mailbox with 10,000 other items trying to sell you something. The distaste is infinitely compounded when risk appears with the message, as in the case of the domestic terrorism problem.

With or without the problem of terrorism, people are pretty fed up with junk mail. The problem is not that these companies are trying to sell products, but that there is no personal relevance to the user. Fortunately this doesn't have to be the case. Be Mary Kay, if only obtusely. By using people, anyone, to endorse the product, you gain a level of credibility and proximity that is much more valuable than any other tool in the fight to sell your product. This does not require huge expenditures on Britney Spears and Zhang Ziyi. In the same way that stars get paid to endorse products, what's wrong with getting ordinary people to endorse a product, especially when everyone wants to be a star anyway?

Sign them up, and get them to talk about a product in a more personal way that gives the audience a connection to a real person, ideally one that identifies with them. A personal Aunt Jemima. But it has to be more than a sticker on the envelope saying, "I loved the product – Tennessee," with a picture of some woman who looks like a WeightWatchers case study, which everyone instantly dismisses as bullshit. Endorsement must be multidimensional and integral to the presentation of what you are trying to sell.

A successful example of this kind of endorsement was Calvin Klein's @ campaign, where the company got ordinary people to host an online forum that was connected to its advertising – publishing e-mail addresses with posters and other printed materials at retail venues around the world. The program generated lots of awareness because Calvin Klein took the time to value ordinary people, turning them into paid spokesmen but not trying to hide the fact that they were CK proxies … valuing them as, at the very least, entertainment for the client audience.

If direct marketers incorporated more of this pitch in their materials, maybe response rates would pick up – a result of trying to connect with people as opposed to just flogging them more products. It's just another way of adding experience to the product equation, in this case by using an audience of peers to flog your product, showing indeed that you do respect your audience.

Keeping with that example, it's a good idea to think about using the second tool, advertising, to connect with that direct mail audience. Harnessing the perceived power of word of mouth will generally be more effective than stating your case directly, even over email. Take the following example:

■ Bad E-mail Marketing

Subject: Increase your erection by 581%
Date: Tuesday, Nov 20, 15:51:23 +0100

Reply | Reply All | Forward | Delete | Previous | Next | Close

SIMPLE PILL CAN INCREASE YOUR EJACULATION By 581%!!!

NO Gimmick........REAL SCIENCE!
Increase Ejaculation by almost 600%!
Increase Sex Drive!
Stronger Erections!
Longer Lasting Orgasms!
More Intense Orgasms!
Shoot up to 13 feet!

New medical breakthrough has now created a
revolutionary herbal pill that is guaranteed to increase
your Semen and EJACULATION by almost 600% in just a
few short weeks! This amazing new product works by
simply taking 2 pills every day... Order Now!

Order Now!
Simply try these Amazing pills for 30 days and if after 30
days you do not experience both a huge increase in the
amount of semen you ejaculate along with longer
lasting more intense orgasms, simply send the empty
bottle back to us and we'll refund you 100% of the cost
including shipping. With this guarantee, our product
must work for you... or we'll lose money on every sale!

– Winner of the BURDETT RESEARCH "GOLDEN STAR" AWARD

ALL NATURAL HERBAL COMPLEX CAPSULE
RESULTS MAY VARY. NOTE: Go to here to be removed.

Nobody, but nobody is ever going to buy this product the way it is presented above. A much more effective strategy would have been for this company, however shambolic it may be, to have gathered a small group of trial users, then developed a direct marketing message around their experience. Then they send that out, both to the people in the network they used and to their rented databases, citing their experiences to sell the viability of the product. This would be less costly and far more effective.

■ OK E-mail Marketing

Subject: TAIPEI
Date: Friday, Nov 9, 09:51:23 +0100

Reply | Reply All | Forward | Delete | Previous | Next | Close

> **We are pleased to announce the launch of FE21 MEGA, the Far Eastern Group's new retail concept department store located in Kaohsiung, Taiwan.**
>
> **FE21 MEGA was created to fulfill the shopping desires of a new generation. The dynamic environment allows for the total shopping experience with improved selections of goods as well as dining and entertainment facilities (Warner Village Cinema) all under one roof.**

The above example has the luxury of being an announcement, while the previous one is trying to directly sell something. It works better in part because it talks to the consumer in a more personal way, as if it is providing a service or some information that may be of value to the consumer. To get to good e-mail marketing, try combining that idea into a hybrid message that is part announcement, part sales call.

A good direct execution will be based on fact but cater to proximity. For reasons of professionalism and good brand reputation, which have proved necessary for survival in hub culture, the message should always be based on fact. This means you cannot cut corners by fabricating the core message.

There should always be a signed agreement for distribution by referenced subjects, whether they are specifically identified or not. Anything else is fraud.

Find a spokesman, make it interesting and let the audience do the work through viral marketing. Not only is this form of direct marketing slightly less annoying than the typical garden variety, it has value as entertainment, however slight. This dramatically increases the service proposition of the product making the message at least vaguely tolerable by a larger portion of the people who have the misfortune of accidentally clicking it open as they sort through their morning in-tray.

Anything else is trash. Actually, this is trash too, but at least it is mildly interesting trash, and respects the consumer enough to call a spade a spade. In a culture where choice is everywhere and baldly stating your message will never get you very far, it's a good idea to let your audience do the work for you. That individual referral, as bought and paid for as a celebrity sponsorship but 1,000 times cheaper, will get you much farther than you ever could go on your own. You are now to step two of the branding and selling proposition: advertising. Getting other people to talk about your product for you.

Remember: "It's about me." To hub culture, stars are really not much more valuable than average people, provided they demonstrate their relevance to them. That connection is achieved through a personal approach that encompasses respect for your audience, and the perception of passing on information, a favor, or simply, a little nugget of entertainment.

Advertising That Works

For companies with "budget," advertising is the primary means of communicating a public message. Effective advertising is often endorsement-linked or linked to fulfilling our spiritual needs via material proxy, which we discussed earlier. The four main forms of advertising are in print, television, online and OOH (out-of-home, or outdoor, like billboards).

Advertising is purchased largely on reach and context. Reach is easy to quantify by a plethora of metrics that have been established to measure advertising and is more related to the cost side. It is formulaic in that there are standard purchase prices for reach determined by these metrics, including syndicated surveys, television ratings systems, and alphabet soup print research like MRI, EMS and ATMS. It has online sisters in PeopleMeter and NetMetrics, the online standards.

Reach is also a function of pure mathematical equations of CPM (cost per thousand), taking the cost of advertising and dividing by the circulation of a magazine or the number of cable subscribers or the number of households in the footprint of a satellite. Online advertising is increasingly purchased on sales delivery but still operates on similar principles extended from reach and price basics. OOH is purchased either for broad impact or narrow point of sale association, and again pricing here is determined by the size of the audience it reaches. Broad impact is measured by potential audience and calculated accordingly, taking into account wastage, while point-of-sale pricing often deals with the direct sales result associated with a particular outlet or venue. Understanding reach is easy, because it is mathematically driven.

Context offers more room for manipulation than reach, which means more opportunity for marketers to shape the impact of their message to their key targets. Buying on context thus offers more room for connection to the spiritual side of branding than reach.

Context is the stuff surrounding the ad, formed by the editorial environment that makes up the product – a TV show, a magazine, news. As such, context is important to the statement you are trying to make with your advertising. Companies advertise in *I.D.*, a cult British-style bible, because it is known for cutting-edge analysis of the fashion world that breaks old *Cosmopolitan* conventions in favor of a gritty, subculture-driven worldview. *I.D.* has achieved great success by flouting convention, even thumbing its nose at advertisers, in an attempt to connect with an anti-establishment readership. Advertisers find this valuable because it helps them connect their brand with that readership as well. Context effectively says, "this content is what our brand is about," however vaguely.

Context makes positioning important. First there is the hierarchy of who goes first, second and third at the front of the book, a pecking order of dominance that is more about the relationships of competitive companies to each other than the actual consumer. Companies in a leadership position expect to be positioned in the magazine ahead of their rivals. Companies not in a leadership position want to be positioned next to the leading companies in an attempt to be seen in the same league. This is part of why there is always such a rush toward particular titles at certain times. When a few leaders decide a title is worth buying, everyone else also rushes in. This gives inordinate control to the biggest spenders and supports arguments for big ad budgets. Image is everything, and the ability to be out there says a lot about how strong a company is relative to its competitors.

There is also a fight for adjacencies that ties to a particular message the advertiser wants to be associated with. If it is a business title, maybe it wants to be associated with a certain columnist or a regular series on technology. If it's a general weekly, maybe the advertiser wants to tie in to the travel section or the health section – wherever it can increase the chance that a reader interested in that content will also be interested in the product. This works across categories, whether you are selling hotel rooms or mouthwash.

There are many forms of advertising, but the most effective advertising will appeal to the spiritual side we have discussed so much, and if it can compliment the intelligence of the audience, so much the better. We discussed the global strategy appeal to hub culture of companies like Sephora, but it works on a wider scale too. Here, Target is a fantastic example.

The Target campaign employs all the basics of great advertising: it is a simple, image-oriented campaign that conveys the core function of the business while speaking to the audience with a level of respect. It is culturally fresh, in a homogenized David LaChapelle sort of way, and it has the potential to leave a cultural impression as deep as the Absolut Vodka campaign, a campaign that single handedly made Absolut into a loved, global brand.

Target's success with its ads has been so complete that it has raised the company to a new level in the consumer psyche, so much that hub culture jokingly refers to it as "Tar-zhay," employing a French pronunciation that means "this brand has gone way upscale, even though it's really not".

For the benefit of those blind cave-dwellers out there who have not run across Target's distinctive campaign, it is terribly simple. The consumer product emporium employed a series of color-driven executions with visual scenarios made up of products available at its retail locations. They work well in both TV and print, but for the purposes of this example I will focus on the print.

The first, a red ad, featured a red lawn and a red house with a red fence and photogenic people dressed in red. The kicker was that all of the features were made of common household brands, in a gingerbread-house style that was quirky and oh-so-sarcastic. Following the red ad came green and yellow and orange, complete with walls of Tide laundry soap. The campaign quickly found seasonal extensions, such as Christmas white, with a snowboard made of Crest logos and boxes of Dove soap hanging as ornaments from a white tree.

The beauty of the campaign was Target's implicit assumption that the consumer is already educated. We all know we are surrounded by these brands, we consume them and we have a relationship with them. Instead of trying to sell the same way, it decided to use their ubiquity to poke an inside joke at the products themselves, saying in effect – "Listen, you know you gotta have this stuff, we sell it, and you know that. So what can we do to have fun with it?"

By expressing the products as pop culture, Target does far more to build its brand and the featured products as must-have, fashionable items. Dove soap is not fashionable. Dove soap as Christmas ornaments is at least … interesting. In this case, the ads create their own context, but that context is supported by where the ads were placed – in high-end consumer magazines such as *Vogue*, *Wallpaper** and *Vanity Fair*. The context these magazines provide made the final connection between the products to lifestyle and fashion. The fact that they ran globally also did much to raise awareness of Target throughout the hubs, so much so it has already gained momentum should it decide to open in Tokyo or Beijing. People in these markets are aware of the brand, they think it is fun, and they'll shop when the stores open.

The ads are also core to the long-term strategy of Target. Unlike Kmart, which filed for bankruptcy, Target realized that it will have trouble competing with Wal-Mart, its core competitor, on price alone. Even if Target does match on price, the perception persists that Wal-Mart is the category killer on price. Target also realized that most consumers (especially hub consumers, who influence those downstream markets) would be a shade embarrassed to be seen in Kmart or Wal-Mart. By developing such an aggressive campaign, it shifted the perception of the brand, and amazingly, Target did it in under a year. It also infected the culture, to such an extent that it affects its design and store aesthetic, leading to deals with "cool" international designers like Michael Graves and Philippe Starck (admittedly making them a bit "over," but which boosted Target by a mile). The fundamental result is that hub consumers are not embarrassed to be seen in Target. It's simply cooler than the competition. Kate, an urban girl who lives in New York and Asia, said it best: "Before the campaign I wouldn't be caught dead. It's gained a downtown credibility – like searching for flea market finds. It's acceptable to accessorize from Target, not Wal-Mart." For Target, that's HUGE.

PR

Trust is the foundation of good PR, but gossip is its fuel. In much the same way that direct marketing has to appeal to the individual and advertising has to respect the audience, successful PR is built around trust and credibility, with a hint of spice. Inherently, this takes time to establish, but the good news is that when applied strategically, it can be done without great financial expense, especially if you can find a newsy, insider angle to your message.

As in the cocktail party anecdote, the best PR is going to be word-of-mouth discussions that grow between the groups of users who consume a product or interact with a brand. One way to foster those discussions is to create a forum for them to speak, or an event around which people gather. For example, the forum could be a referral program that provides incentives to existing clients to tell others about a product or service. In hub culture individual credibility is at stake with every recommendation, so a positive mention can be taken very seriously. This does tremendous benefit to the brand in question. The downside is that a negative mention can be twice as damaging.

It is best to have this kind of PR develop organically, like from a really hot product or a sales person who is so fantastic with her clients that word spreads among others, who seek her out. Fortunately, where such luxuries do not exist, this kind of PR can be manufactured.

It is a three step process:

[1] Identify a point of differentiation about the subject in question that makes it unique (yes, we are back to oddity, which also adds value as discussed in chapter 2).

[2] Find a way to express that point as a bit of news or information that has no obvious benefit to the self-interest of the company or the product.

[3] Talk up that angle to gain momentum behind it from outside sources, especially by cross-fertilizing it among unrelated opinion leaders.

An extreme, if accidental example of this is seen in the Simpson's, which constantly riffs on Fox, its owner, by making fun of it. Somehow, that makes Fox seem cooler than if the Simpson's were actually plugging Fox with a compliment.

A more basic example of this kind of PR thinking is evidenced in the ongoing Beetle campaign. As early as 1994, Volkswagen was showing the Beetle in Berlin and talking it up specifically to the auto industry. The key message regarded not the design or the function, as much as its retro appeal. The retro appeal is the point of news or information that had no obvious benefit to the company but which was interesting to those who make buzz. The buzz started, and it was as much about the IDEA behind the new Beetle as much as it was about the look or function of the car itself.

The next step after identifying these points is to get the message out, and here it is best to do a combination approach that couples press releases and bulletins with face-to-face communication to key industry targets – such as trade publications or other stakeholders and hawks in your industry. By getting their buy-in first, they can do a lot of the work for you in getting the message you want out to the market when a product launch or other product coverage comes along. This is very important, and a good strategy is to ring your priorities outward from the company to the end consumer – taking into account the various layers of people who influence the discussion about the product or service.

As such, you have quite a few people to talk to in the PR world before you actually start talking to your consumer or buyer. Keep in mind that the function of PR is less to talk to the buyer, that is the job of direct marketing. Instead, it's a bit like spritzing the air with the fragrance of your presence. Smelling good comes from attention to integrity and reputation.

This becomes vastly more important to have in place when something smelly comes by, as it invariably will. By continually spritzing the air with PR messages and that overall glow of trust and goodness, people are less likely to notice other smells. Or at least not as quickly, which gives you more time to try and clean them up.

A few small ancillary points about PR:

[1] Where possible, collect and maintain e-mail addresses for key decision-makers, and make sure all press releases go out over e-mail as well as fax to the major news services or your category trade publications. This e-mail angle is vitally important, because your way of speaking is much more likely to be picked up by journalists when they can cut and paste part of your release. And believe me, they do.

[2] Consider hosting a regular function that ties to some aspect of

your business for the key buzz makers in your world. Not a splashy, corporate-driven affair that people get invited to all the time, but a handwritten personal invitation to join you for cocktails or a seminar or whatever. This goes such a long way to improve the level of sincerity without having to take them out individually, which will cost more and eat up more time. When you think about who to invite, consider who THEIR influentials are and decide if they fit on your invite list. Where their influentials are, they are likely to be as well.

[3] Experience. Where possible, enable the target to experience the product or service you offer. If your business is a furniture store or a spa, look at doing an "influentials" tour for the buzzmakers in the community that gives them the full treatment. Nothing persuades like experience.

Reaching the Hub

Even though they are geographically diverse, one thing the people who define hub culture have in common is a constant interaction with the main hubs – the cities that are the foundation of hub culture. Many of them live there, but even those who live outside the hubs at least travel to and from them. As such, a geographically urban strategy will produce the best results with the least investment. Find PR people in several hubs who know their market personally, and concentrate advertising in media that filters across hubs.

A good branding strategy will link the tools, direct marketing, advertising and PR, with exposure strategies that span the main cities. To reach the hubs, link the tools to the poles, travel and communication, and base the message around the aspects of their lifestyle with regard to work, leisure and relationships.

Provided that you are doing image or reputation branding, it is easy to employ a consistent message with these tools because the product message itself is less specific. For the travel pole, you can target airports, hotels, upscale boutiques, cafés and clubs, and regional or global publications that have an appeal to the hub. This will be much less expensive than developing simultaneous local campaigns that employ a larger portion of local publications or outdoor advertising.

When looking at retail and other ventures, keep in mind that urban centers are where the personality of individual hubs develops, and the point where context benefits can be applied to a real world setting. By choosing flagships in urban centers, you can build a global brand with just a few stores. Fred Segal, Nobu and Mikimoto are great examples of this in practice.

Additionally, think about reaching the hubs through their communication channels. This could include SMS and m-commerce programs, web-based advertising and direct mail, or trying to find a way to reach them on the desktop or personal communicator, but not necessarily through the web – such as a content link-up with companies like SonyEricsson, (or their resellers and content providers) incentive offers with telecom carriers and credit-card companies.

If you want local media in the mix, think about city guides and other items that the hubs refer to when they travel and when they want to know what is going on in their own city. Online, the e-mail portals offer regular access for brand building, but global sites that appeal to adventure sports, fashion and other luxury goods coverage, spirituality and theosophical-oriented information sites, and on a wider scale, news sites, seem to be where the hubs migrate most.

When the message has to be product focused, the obvious need for market localization will exist. But when targeting the hubs you can still frame the message in the context of the group's attributes, even across relatively dissimilar products. Here is where focused PR will do a lot of good, because it allows you to get other people talking about specific products without you having to spend as much in promotion through more expensive media channels. Focused PR will include product sampling and placement initiatives. For placement, consider local hub personalities who are internationally oriented, such as those associated with popular restaurants or hotels, spas and sports – the micro stars that make each city a little brighter. Not only will they be much less expensive, but their role in influencing their groups will generate that sought-after ripple effect that flows out across wider society.

chapterfourteen
The Future in General

No one can predict the future, but a few things seem to be on the cards:
[1] Consumer China is the next America.
[2] America and Japan are swimming against the same tide.
[3] Europe is in brain-drain danger, but fortunately it's a nice place to visit.
[4] The hub cities, being common in their new cultural identity, mitigate these new regional realities.
[5] Within the hub cities, the next-generation company is taking shape, driven by the primary demand of the hub: ubiquitous, end-to-end service across a variety of products and activities.

These are broad and sweeping points of reference, but they play a role in the way we think about the hubs and the larger regional or national considerations that affect the hub's ability to fully participate in the new market. It also affects how we market, and where we put our focus and our resources for the best strategic return. I will take a few minutes to explain what meaning exists in these regional shifts, followed by the role individual hubs are playing within and between the regions. These shifts are not absolutely defined by the hubs, but the personalities and emphasis within the hubs will evolve in tandem with these regions, even as they all grow closer and closer together in their common expression and outlook.

Then we'll look at how companies are evolving to deal with the new common market and outline the structure of the "neocompania," an evolving corporate structure that makes brands proxies for everything material, however unrelated, targeted to the culture with which they are primarily engaged.

The Big Picture: Hub Cities in Development

Emma is the head of marketing at Dunhill, Asia Pacific. "China is the new Japan," she said over lunch one day as we discussed the commercial prospects for the English luxury men's retailer in the near term. Her comment was specific to her business, and this is true in the high-end luxury sector. But in a broader sense she understands that China is the new America. Japan, for the luxury goods category, has been the giant gorilla gobbling up sales and fueling the category's global expansion, much as America has been the gorilla buyer for the rest of the world economy, especially over the last 10 years. The next big buyer in the global economy, whether the sector is handbags or autos or architecture, is China. It's also the next big seller.

On a wider scale, one could say that Asia in general is the next big player because of the population equation, although a number of scholars have argued that China is in danger of collapse, decay or revolution. All of these things may be true, but the momentum has started for China, fueled by collapsing walls of information, and it would be very surprising to see it turn course from the route for which it has sailed. As the playing field levels, education improves and China focuses on building itself, inwardly (much as America did in the early 20th century), its force will be unmistakable. Executives from strategy consultant Bain & Company sum it up concisely: "China now is where the US was in the 1890s, but the development is much more accelerated." Just like McDonald's, 1.2 billion people can't be wrong.

Japan will continue to be a force in both innovation and adaptation for many sectors, and as a consumer market its size and wealth remain a potent force, even if it is a force receding in scale to the avalanche of Chinese buying that is already shoring up the accounting books of consumer retailers, especially in the high-end sector.

According to Emma and other fashion retailers, fully 80% of global revenues from companies like LVMH, Hermés, PPR (Gucci, YSL) come from Japan. At Gucci, the number for Asia is about half of total revenues, but that does not account for Japanese traveling to other markets to buy, which is included in Emma's number. Most of the money going to the luxury houses has not come from Japanese buying in the stores that now line the Ginza, but from Japanese who traveled and scooped up bargains in Sydney, Honolulu and Paris, fueling those economies. Back in the mid '90s, it was not uncommon for Japanese tour agents to charter commercial planes full of shoppers to fly to these places (even duty free outposts like Guam), lugging the loot back to Japan.

Sometimes it was sold as a parallel import, but more often, it was just a good excuse for people to save money – buying in Paris, even with the airfare, was still cheaper than shopping for half the selection at twice the price in Tokyo. When the Japanese stopped traveling, the luxury goods retailers responded by opening huge stores all over Japan – Sapporo, Osaka ... everywhere, to cater to the huge Japanese market. Tokyo remains the showcase for these brands, capped by the Louis Vuitton global store, JCrew super stores, the earlier mentioned mega-amazing Hermés building, and others, many around the Ginza and Harajuku prefectures.

To Americans, understanding the old Japanese method of travel-to-shop behavior is generally a little bit difficult, but that is because Americans don't understand what it's like to pay duties of 200% on imported goods. It also tends to conjure up parallel images of Versace-clad Venezuelan drug-lord wives leaving on the 06:55 a.m. from Caracas, flying to Miami for a day of shopping and lunch on the bay, only to return on the red-eye back south. There is a certain amount of, uh, extravagance to that form of consumption. After 12 years of post-bubble yuk-enomics and a slight reduction in the duties, most Japanese came to realize that it was a bit extravagant too, and even though there is unrelenting demand for the latest, most avant-garde, they are a little less likely to globe-trot for the Fendi alligator than they used to.

Despite the Japan factor, the big prize is China. At last count, Dunhill had over 60 stores in China, compared to nine in America. This is where Dunhill is placing its bets, and in the luxury category, so is everyone else. Burberry, Louis Vuitton, Prada, Salvatore Ferragamo, (even mass retailers like Wal-Mart and IKEA) all say their future growth is inextricably linked to success in China. Interestingly, the near-term growth is in secondary cities like Dalian and Chengdu, where second-tier status as a city translates into first-tier desires by the residents. In Dalian, people want the status of the genuine article. In Shanghai, they are already ambivalent and just as likely to accept a fake one at a lower price.

In the auto industry the growth story is much the same: BMW, DaimlerChrysler, Fiat and Ford are all working on joint ventures with Chinese companies to start building cars for the Chinese market, and the success of Volkswagen and General Motors in their China JV projects has given them cause for hope that the investments they are making now, even if for just a piece of the future action, are not only worthwhile, but necessary to their long-term viability in the global market.

But even though luxury companies are eyeing the China market thinking it is becoming a source of huge demand and profits, the auto companies are more on the mark, for they seem to realize that in the long run the Chinese market will probably more closely resemble the American market. The reason is not just size – with one out of every four planetary citizens in China it's news to nobody that the consumer demand rivaling America will eventually be there.

The similarity is in the development and tastes of consumerism, combined with the wider spaces and the ambitions of the country itself, which lend a closer parallel to the US in the path of its development. Even the consumers in China tend to be a bit more conservative – more like the Americans, less consumed with fads, more into classic cuts and quality and price, unlike the Japanese who tend to put more emphasis on the frivolous part of frivolous. Of course, China is huge and widely disparate, so parts are comparable to Japan. Already, China enjoys more than 18 million millionaires, which is more than the entire population of Australia. China can definitely do frivolous exceptionally well.

Since China is also less developed than Japan and quite hungry for new ideas, the ability to leapfrog other countries by employing the latest infrastructure and technologies leaves increasing room for companies that wish to participate in segments of the economy where there are not strongly established domestic players. Since most of the economy was or is state-run, additional opportunities exist from partnership with newly privatized initiatives or special economic development projects that trade expertise for equity. The end result is a more open strategy for market entry.

America and Japan are both swimming against the same tide – trying to wring growth from stagnant markets as their populations age. One of the great fears by economists in both markets is what will happen as baby boomers begin to withdraw from the consumer markets, a trend that will accelerate in the middle of the decade as they begin to hit retirement, or at least pass their prime earning years. The only balance will be to continue looking outside their home markets to invest and to sell – markets bursting with younger populations across the developing world. Places like Brazil, with improving infrastructure and heaps of young people, stand out.

Since consumers in these economies have already been cultivated and harvested – both exploited and maximized in their value, the eternal search for growth is an incentive for companies based there to increasingly build outside their national borders. Both markets are mature in an economic sense, and enjoy bursts of organic growth only with technological innovation and the cyclical needs of the business sector. In turn, the business sector is itself constantly fighting a war of over-and-under capacity that generates a near zero sum return in the long run.

Europe faces the same maturation problems as Japan and America, but is saddled with the additional pressure of structural rigidity in its economies and a preoccupation with the past that is less obvious in Asia and America. The continued integration of the European Union provides a focal point for the future, but it can't seem to get past the fact that many Europeans find the best chance for wealth generation in markets abroad. Sometimes that just means going to London, Europe's main hub, but often it means Asia, where the big infrastructure and consumer development needs offer more lucrative deals. Airbus, for instance, is banking on Asia and Russia for future growth of the air transport industry, resulting in a big focus on advertising and marketing targeted to that region.

The key in Europe remains the integration of ethnicity and multiculturalism to decreasingly national populations. The changes that have occurred in Paris and Berlin and London over the last ten years – fueled by a growing acceptance of ethnicity as a cultural advantage, are helping to foster new innovation, but this seems limited to the hubs. Outside, among the broader populations, dangers of racial fundamentalism and intolerance still hold some sway.

The Mind Race: Hub Corporations in Development

Over coffee at Starbucks with an Australian marketer, David, we got to talking about multinational branding. He thinks from an anthropological perspective, while my viewpoint stems from an economics background. The funny thing about hub culture is that half the people are so well educated or have such extensive experience working in the international arena that it doesn't take much to get them to share their thoughts, as everyone likes to think they are the expert on SOMETHING. David is no exception.

Anyway, David contributed the following salient point about brands: "Product lines are blurring and brands are consolidating quickly, especially under a series of a few holding companies that tout synergy as their raison d'etre." This means that US, German, British and other companies are becoming like Japanese *kieretsus* and Korean *chaebols,* with accompanying dangers of conflict of interest and insular thinking that America so haughtily sniffs at Japan and Korea about on a regular basis. Currently, we don't think of Nike, Disney, LVMH and HSBC as competitors. Nike makes shoes and apparel as part of a larger sporting universe strategy. Disney operates in the entertainment field, LVMH is in luxury image goods and HSBC is a financial services leader. But the fight for survival in our hyper-competitive, cluttered ad environment means that all four of these companies are beginning to compete for one identical thing: the consumer's time, attention and eventually, heart. What you sell is becoming secondary to how you access your target. When the product a brand sells is no longer the primary motivator to the sale, the company can essentially sell anything ... and will, as long as they can compete effectively in either quality or scarcity through additional service.

The true implications of this have only just begun to unravel, but they will fundamentally change the way we view brands over the next few years – what a company makes or sells is less important than how you as a consumer feel about the company, because the big brands will sell you such a wide variety of goods and services that their traditional product lines of, say, shoes and apparel and sporting accessories are viewed as just another revenue stream. Operating by the product you sell is narrow thinking, as obsolete as thinking a cereal company can only sell one kind of cereal.

Twenty years ago no one thought it was appropriate for Nike to sell anything besides shoes, but the brand became strong enough that it eventually moved into apparel, with success. From there, it went into accessories and light sporting goods, quite a far cry from footwear, in an attempt to build an overall sports-related identity. Next up, Nike TV, a media project that puts it into competition with every media company that produces content or sells advertising. Especially because of the lower cost of entry due to the Internet, media has been the first industry to be affected by this explosion of offerings – every large consumer brand is now starting to behave in some way like a media company.

After media comes financial services and planning, with a wide variety of sophisticated finance mechanisms that allows the purchase of big-ticket items, non-cash payment for smaller items, sophisticated barter and trade systems between corporations themselves, and electronic micro-payment initiatives. All allow traditional product-oriented companies to add finan-cial services (however silent) to their necessary competencies. Large corpo-rations already do this behind the scenes to improve efficiency in their fi-nancial statements, making trades on their stock, buying shares in other companies and investing in emerging markets to manage their money. Even-tually this will bleed out to consumers on the financial retail side. The larg-est, most successful brands will offer these financial services – much the way GM already finances sales of cars and trucks, and the way mass retailers offer store-branded credit cards to loyal customers. Offering these addi-tional services again allows these corporations to up the ante on the quality, service and scarcity equation that is so fundamental to preserving price. All this is done to avoid commoditization of their core businesses.

There are three factors driving the development of the wide-range brand: global outsourcing, economies of scale and the loyalty/productivity relationship.

Outsourcing

As discussed previously, these days anybody can make anything, for a price. The technology behind most mid-value consumer products is widely avail-able, and manufacturing processes are transparent. If HSBC decides it wants to make toasters to give as an incentive to its banking clients, it takes about 10 minutes to get an order placed. When Gucci decided that snorkel equip-ment and volleyballs would be a fun spring/summer accessory, it simply had them made.

Across most consumer goods industries, actual manufacturing and pro-duction of everything from luxury watches to computer circuit boards have consolidated to a few global players. If a brand wants to make something, it simply calls up a manufacturing partner and requests the item, or gives them the specific designs created by outsourced specialists like the style-trackers. The supplier then pushes the button on production with any number of companies that are pumping out similar products, many of which are in China, Japan and other parts of Asia.

The eyewear and watch industries illustrate the point. If you are Max Mara, Ralph Lauren, Burberry, or Donna Karan, you have an alliance with an Italian company called Safilo, which has a large portion of the global eyewear market. Safilo receives designs every season from the brands, and works with its own networks of factories (from Europe to Asia), to produce hundreds of thousands of pieces under label for these brands. Some go back to the individual companies for sale in their own stores and distribution through their private channels. The remainder of the production is disseminated across Safilo's own network of thousands of eyewear retailers, who carry dozens of brands in a single shop.

Safilo's main competitor is Luxottica, which has the majority of the market and operates on a very similar structure. Together they account for upwards of 70% of the mid- to upper-range eyewear market. A few smaller players, such as Rayban and No Fear produce as well, though they are less likely to act as an outsourcer as Safilo or Luxottica. All also have their own brands and lines they are working to expand and develop.

The moment that BMW decides it wants to launch a line of high-performance driving eyewear, it can conceivably do it very quickly. Both Safilo and Luxoticca could, if pressed, handle not only the production but the design and distribution for BMW, ensuring that BMW is able to roll out a top-notch product, despite the fact that BMW knows zilch about eyewear. BMW eyewear may sound unlikely, but who would have ever thought Porsche would have a successful luggage business, or that Samsonite would be making some of today's trendiest clothes?

The outsourcing scenario is playing itself out now across all industries. TAG Heuer, the famous Swiss watchmaker, isn't actually a watchmaker – it's a marketing company that outsources much of the production of its watches to a prestigious collection of Swiss master watchmakers separate from the actual company. Granted, they are very good, but they are not guaranteed to be TAG Heuer employees.

Louis Vuitton uses Loewe workers in Spain to work on its leather products, and has been known to completely outsource the production of some items, especially when demand is so strong that its own craftsmen can't complete orders. It should be noted that there is a matter of degree to this kind of outsourcing, especially with regard to luxury companies and their bigger-ticket items. Louis Vuitton would never outsource to Asia, even though the quality of production is often just as good, because it would be ruined if anyone ever found out the company was producing a $2,000 briefcase in Bangladesh. The quality may not be affected, but the image it cultivates would be greatly tarnished, because there is no romantic association with Bangladesh in the mind of the consumer like there is with the crafting traditions of Europe.

Since Loewe's Spanish workers are actually among the world's best, other luxury goods companies, including those not related to Loewe under the LVMH brand, also use them to produce certain leather items. And since production facilities are not as elastic as demand, Loewe sells leather goods to other companies to use and distribute as their own at a tidy profit. Loewe will generally refuse to put the Loewe name on the item to protect the impression it conveys from its own brand. Both Loewe and Louis Vuitton are also careful to employ distinctions that make their particular products unique. In the leather world it's all about the grain. Only Louis Vuitton has "real" epi-leather, a watermark imprint placed on the leather that gives that line a distinguished look. Loewe also insists on certain leathers and unique leather stampings that only it can use, to create a subtle difference to its product. Both also make sure that no one else can buy the exact same leather, even from certain geographic locations within Europe. Most consumers don't know this, but they also don't know that Loewe sometimes makes Vuitton either.

The bottom line is that the same person could be making your leather wallet, regardless of what label it ends up with. The flip side to this is that you can buy your leather wallet, eyewear and snorkeling equipment from the same label, should you so choose. This horizontal ability to cross sell is at the core of success in the move for companies to embrace "lifestyle" as their key selling point.

The outsourcing trend is clear everywhere a product or service is produced, from autos that are made in collaboration among different car companies and sold under different marques, all the way down to the toys in a Happy Meal, which are produced by the same handful of companies that make the action figures for Mattel, which are the same companies that churn out licensed product for Disney and Warner Brothers.

Economies of Scale

This massive move toward outsourcing creates two layers of business functionality defined by our old dot-com era buzzwords, business-to-business and business-to-consumer. Business-to-consumer brands become purveyors of anything and everything, while business-to-business producers and manufacturers become ever more specialized, spitting out variations of the same products for a variety of companies. Economies of scale drive both sides: The larger quantities that the manufacturers produce allow them to do so at a lower cost per unit, helping them on price. As we all know, all things being equal, the supplier will often get screwed on price, as the client whittles down the margin by threatening to use other suppliers who can offer the same goods or services at a lower price. The bigger the manufacturer becomes, the more it tries to consolidate its position by leading in technology and speed to market – factors that help alleviate pricing pressure that would be absolute if it was just about who could produce what by when.

Similarly, companies have two ways in which they can move to build their economies of scale: horizontally, across other product categories in an effort to build market share or enter parallel markets; or vertically, in an attempt to control as many points along the value chain as possible, from start to finish in the conception, production, distribution, sale and maintenance of a consumer product. Different companies have different strategies, but it seems that brands move best horizontally, not vertically. This is true despite the fact that many CEOs will tell you that they are moving their companies vertically in an attempt to rein in costs and improve quality of their branded products.

For the brands, leading in innovation (technology) and speed to market are key factors in enabling them to command a price premium from the consumer. This goes back to our ongoing discussion about quality and scarcity. Innovation and technology improvements affect the quality of the brand's products, while speed to market ensures that you can control scarcity, if only for a limited time. Applied across a range of products, a multiplier effect takes hold that encourages brands to diversify their product offerings as much as possible to cover hits and misses. That way, if silk ties are out of favor you have a hit in mobile phone covers to fall back on, as Dunhill learned in collaboration with Nokia.

That is a mid-range example, but like those little Russian dolls you see all over tourist locations in the Caribbean, the pattern repeats itself all the way up and down the economic food chain. At the top, the biggest companies, like Sony, Microsoft, and AOL Time Warner are all looking at trying to dominate and blur the lines of what they offer: content, products, entertainment, services ... Microsoft's move into hardware with the Xbox, combined with its move into entertainment with NBC and MSN and, probably soon, financial services with General Electric, complement alliances with partners who provide specialized information.

The simultaneous business-to-business and business-to-consumer relationships apply similarly across many categories. In this instance, Forbes, which produces electronic business and financial information for itself as well as for MSN, can be compared to Loewe. These wildly different companies have the same model. Both produce their own product, available in Loewe shops or in *Forbes* and at forbes.com. Yet they also sell some product (business news, leather) to others – whether Louis Vuitton or Microsoft, for additional revenue or as a promotional extension into those larger companies' product mix.

In addition, there is a mirror effect to economies of scale. The same suppliers and manufacturers who are busy specializing and growing for economy of scale on one side are often outsourcing their own internal business processes to be able to offer their range of clients a fuller suite of end-to-end solutions, again for greater economy of scale. Yesterday's tire-maker is today's tire, rubber glove and glue gum supplier, probably with a stake in the Indonesian rubber plantations that it buys from. It may own limited hard assets core to its primary function, such as the factory equipped to produce the tires, but it also knows how to get you the gloves when you need them.

Within the tire company itself, it may use outsourcing to achieve greater economies of scale, sending out advertising and public relations, human resources, information technology, or other traditional segments of the company to allow the organization to focus resources on building economy of scale in its front-end business; offering a wider variety of services and production of finished goods in the rubber sector.

But an all-everything-all-the-time strategy can harbor risk, because it is really easy for brands to wipe out when they diversify product lines too much or too quickly. It is difficult to achieve success horizontally, but even more difficult to do vertically, where a company decides to move up and down the production chain.

Chiquita (which recently filed for Chapter 11) probably would not suggest going into the processed frozen fruit and ice cream market when your core competency is growing and shipping bananas – (OK, and printing those fun little Carmen Miranda stickers). Chiquita spent the 1990s working on a move into the processed foods market and other vertical development projects that ultimately were not in the best interests of the company or its shareholders. Even though Chiquita enjoyed great brand recognition and a solid revenue base from a large share of the fresh fruit market in bananas and pineapples, its core competency was not in the packaging and sale of processed foods; it was in the growth and transportation of raw food materials.

In hindsight it would be easy to say that it was impossible for a growing and distribution company like Chiquita to move vertically in the food business, supplying more of the end-to-end product development equation. Moving horizontally, a potentially more successful strategy, would have meant expanding into the raw production of other foodstuffs; like trying to corner the lettuce market. Or it could have grown existing market share by investing in more efficient delivery processes that would lower its cost of production.

Even though managing a banana plantation and selling Popsicles are pretty disparate businesses, Chiquita's failure with this particular vertical extension lies less with diversification and attempting to grow its economies of scale than with the method in which the company went about it. If Chiquita thought of itself as a brand first and foremost, it would have outsourced and taken the profits from letting someone else, like Kraft, produce frozen fruit Popsicles under the Chiquita name, harnessing the efficiencies that Kraft has developed over the years in the production of processed food.

Generally, wipeouts come when brands take their eye off the ball on either innovation/quality or speed-to-market/scarcity. They need the size and scope to dominate, but if they don't manage it well, they will end up third in three categories as opposed to first in one. In the current economy, being third just isn't good enough, as Chiquita learned the hard way. The list of companies that have suffered similar wipeouts goes far beyond "C," but for many it comes down to diversifying the wrong way, either outsourcing to the wrong people the wrong way, or by trying to do it all in-house and making a mess of it.

One obvious company that has been great at these brand extensions is Virgin. From telephone space to airlines to cola, the Virgin model always treats the brand as its most valuable asset, leaving the gunky work to the suppliers who specialize in producing and distributing particular products.

Virgin Mobile, available in Australia, offers a wonderful example of how companies are catching on to being everything to everybody. The company offers cellular service in this market by buying bulk time from other cellular providers, rearranging benefits that the average consumer would find appealing, such as fixed rates across all times, and resells it at a price which is competitive to the other telcos, taking advantage of its economy of scale in the purchase of bulk minutes. Virgin is in an enviable position here – it offers an enhanced service by simply repackaging an existing contract, and the company avoids the responsibility of building networks or other capital and time-intensive endeavors, leaving that to its network of suppliers.

Richard Branson's ability to sell his brand, at a premium, for any number of goods and services is exactly where everybody else is starting to head – from Nike to HSBC to Disney. This model is similar to the much-maligned old Korean *chaebols* and Japanese *kieretsus*, groups of independently operating companies living under the same corporate umbrella. This style of thinking is central to companies that have been successful in reaching the hub culture, and rumors of radical brand extensions periodically pop up in the hub community, latching on to the collective psyche with ideas that stretch the old rules of convention but seem perfectly logical to the group. Case in point:

Subject: My kind of flight
Date: Friday, 7 Dec, 15:25:36 +0800

Reply | Reply All | Forward | Delete | Previous | Next | Close

From Clark Howard travel email...

London–based dance music company Ministry of Sound says it has plans to turn passenger jets into flying nightclubs. The company plans to obtain four jets formerly used by Ansett, Australia's second largest airline that recently went bust. Late evening flights are planned between Sydney and Melbourne with special DJ decks where the business class used to be.

In reality, the above e-mail was kind of a hub joke, never to be taken seriously, but it appeared in many "real" news reports. What better combination of hub icons could there be? Travel, lifestyle and entertainment, all wrapped into one neat little package that is itself a transport product between hubs. What was really funny was Ministry of Sound publishing a list of news outlets that "fell" for the joke in a 2002 music compilation.

Regardless, the instant acceptance of the idea by the popular press and companies like Clark Howard demonstrates the lengths to which the new breed of hub company will go to extend its brand into new product lines and more importantly how quickly it can be embraced by the hubs. Moving from dance emporium to transport specialist seems like a wide departure, but in the view of the horizontal and vertical development model it actually makes sense. It is simply offering another service, most of which can be outsourced, and leveraging the Ministry of Sound concept, the culture of the company, to others who run the mechanics of that business. Qantas could never launch a product like this, even Branson would be hard pressed, but because Ministry of Sound has credibility in its specialization, entertainment, it is taken seriously when it takes steps to leverage entertainment into horizontal categories.

If, like Chiquita, it had chosen to expand into construction of the nightclubs it owns and production of the vodka it sells inside, that might be more of a stretch – a vertical leap that would fail, because Ministry of Sound is good at entertaining club kids, not construction and distilling. On the other hand, it would not be hard to brand a vodka as a Ministry of Sound Vodka, and have someone like Diego or Pernod Ricard produce the actual product. This is what fcuk did when it launched its new fcuk Spirits line – expanding the brand from clothing to alcohol in one quick ad campaign. It's lifestyle.

Loyalty/Productivity Relationship

The third leg of this corporate expansion troika is an intertwined story of the relationship between loyalty and productivity, both of which enable companies and brands to achieve more with less, leaving room for expansion into ever wider, ever newer areas with greater chance of success.

Loyalty greatly increases productivity in the world of hub corporations because the cost of acquiring a new customer is usually much greater than the cost of maintaining an existing customer. The more loyal you can make your customers, the more productive your business becomes because you spend less time out hunting for maybes and more time servicing the needs of your existing client base.

It also becomes easier to cross-sell a different product or service to customers you already have a relationship with, which greatly benefits your productivity when you are trying to expand a brand across a number of horizontal points, especially if those points are unrelated in the consumer's mind. But good partners are necessary to effectively navigate these expansions, because the danger of wiping out grows exponentially with such moves.

We've already covered the importance of a good CRM and direct-marketing strategy in the overall marketing mix, and these elements are most important in helping the hub corporation develop loyalty among consumers. Once you have established this loyalty base and an ongoing relationship with the consumer, your customer group is usually more receptive to the introduction of new items through cross-promotion.

A powerful strategic change is underway for businesses that want to court loyalty with their consumers. It has to do with a combination of flexibility and strategic intelligence. Strategic intelligence is the amount of information a company knows about its clients and customers, and increasingly, its competitors. Businesses must be smart and flexible with collective intelligence if they are to be successful in the new century.

For your customer relationship, the challenge in developing strategic intelligence is figuring out how to best harness the data you collect, and how best to turn it into knowledge to make better decisions about what your client base wants. Understanding the knowledge fosters client wisdom. Knowledge also gives a course of action. Information gives you a set of coordinates.

Within companies competitive knowledge is more important than ever, and as companies continually seek competitive advantage, they are increasingly finding guerilla movements (based on flexibility) the best means to gain knowledge of both their customers and their competitors. For customers this is a fine and dangerous line which requires full disclosure if a company is to maintain that halo of good aura that it spends so much time trying to build through other means. If, by using guerilla tactics to acquire information, a company is discovered to have acted improperly, it can be very damaging.

But the cell strategy remains – harmonize the data collection methods over the company, then distribute the responsibility to the tips of the organization, where they collect information and feed it back to the core. This core can then process for trends and common identifiers across the hubs. Meanwhile the ends of the organization use the specific market data they have collected to make individual market decisions.

By centralizing the data on a common platform you are able to forecast and aggregate trends across the hubs, hopefully pointing out where your business is going before it actually gets there. Distributing the work load in a clear template to the cells increases speed because you are increasing the points of the organization that are taking in information, without having to redo everything because data is incompatible. An example of this in practice is to globally harmonize your research so that you can find points of comparison between markets. It doesn't matter what continent or region the market is located in, because the hub market will demonstrate similar characteristics across all of them.

On the competitor information side, there is more scope for employing guerilla tactics. An all-out competitor war doesn't do anyone any favors on brand, price, or research and investment for future progress. But a guerrilla business can use focused cells and stealth to generate localized attacks on larger or smaller competitors. Mastering guerrilla business may in turn be the survival tactic of today's large companies. As big companies morph into cells of largely autonomous action at the local level, they will compete not only against their competitors, but against their parent core and other cells within the organization. This is one way the new European and American kieretsus can avoid the fossilization that has plagued corporate Japan and Korea.

To do this, we must take the superstructure of the company and transform it into a support structure designed to extract the maximum from employees for competitive advantage at the core, while creating a system that feeds and supports local initiatives at the same time. Doing this will cut costs, empower the cells and maximize revenue into the center.

With so much emphasis in big companies on developing this sort of structure, corporate espionage, data mining, profile tracking and consumer monitoring are becoming the new norm, all justified in the name of strategic intelligence. When companies face periodic harsh economic winters, the ability to find competitive advantage through monitoring becomes all the more common.

But there are considerations in the distribution of power throughout the organization, especially if parts of the organization start to veer. Procter & Gamble's 2001 revelation that it had gone dumpster-diving for sales projections from Unilever, in a much talked about but quickly resolved case of corporate espionage, highlights the risks and opportunities companies face with regard to the acquisition of competitive intelligence. This case was about much more than dumpster-diving, and entailed a concerted effort by certain local P&G employees to systematically gather closed proprietary data from Unilever using unconventional means. When the center found out what the cell was doing however, it realized that the implications of the actions would be quite harmful if ever discovered. Thus, P&G blew the whistle on itself. This kind of blow is the downside of too much decentralization, in creating an organizational culture that is very guerilla oriented. Its means surely included more sophisticated techniques than dumpster-diving, many of which were technically legal. But it was still bad business, and P&G knew it. However, from price point and margin information to data on impending launches and new products, securing competitive data, at almost any cost, is the new imperative; especially given this increasingly guerrilla nature of business. The reason? Companies today can actually do something with that data.

Until recently, even if you did go to extraordinary lengths to secure sensitive systemized information from your competitors, it was very difficult to use because it often did not mesh with the scout company's own informational architecture. As corporate monitoring and intellectual theft go from paper-sifting to more sophisticated eavesdropping and photographic monitoring techniques, this constraint of ineffective data is reduced, because electronic data by its nature is far quicker to analyze and compare than plain old sales figures and margin spreads pulled from some trash can.

In response, companies are also going to greater lengths to protect their own electronic data and communications, both from fierce competitors and unwieldy governments. In this sense, they have been operating quietly for many years. One example involves the case of General Motors in China. Today GM is the third largest foreign auto producer in China, in partnership with its local joint venture Shanghai GM. The company was established in the early 1990s to meet foreign entry requirements for auto production within China, but with years to go before entry into the World Trade Organization and a burgeoning population of potential car-buyers, GM saw a JV in China as the future growth vehicle for its checkered international operations.

Key GM executives in China close to the negotiations quickly learned that the Chinese government was listening in on not only the setup negotiations between the JV partner and GM, but GM's own internal communications back to Detroit, which in many cases were highly sensitive. In one of the better noted examples of "James Bond in real life" work scenarios, an executive on the project in Shanghai soon found himself driving to remote locations outside of Shanghai to wait for a satellite link to pass overhead. With an ancestor to the Iridium phone that he would lug out of the boot of his car, he would follow the coordinates, dial at the correct time and relay important information back to Detroit while bypassing Chinese government authorities who may have been very interested to listen in over conventional phone lines.

Given that such tapping would have been illegal in other places, the motive here is self-defense, and given what GM had at stake, the steps the company took to secure communication transmissions from China were justified, even at the high prices such activities command. How long can it be before such actions are normal for companies with an interest in protecting their livelihood, and how long after that before such actions are abused by companies using the technology against each other?

The answer is not very long, but that is the new reality of the hub corporation. It is flat, light, flexible and guerrilla-esque in execution. Kind of like a cockroach.

On the other hand, hub corporations will work to bury this internal side of the business with an ever-increasing focus on corporate reputation, honor and reliability – all factors of survival in a world where communication is instant and hub consumers are fickle. The more they develop the brands in their efforts to communicate with the hub, the more they will have to espouse the virtues of a higher ideal to remain relevant. They have to keep up with their consumer.

Micro-brands

"I won't work with someone I don't know and trust. The most important assets of my company are my reputation, my contacts and my ability to connect people." – *Deborah, media consultant*

A word on micro-brands, a style of company that is developing quickly in many globalized industries, especially fashion and media. Micro-brands are in many ways the corporate expression of the nonjob job worker – the individuals who increasingly fill the cracks between large companies intently focused on outsourcing. The hallmark of the micro-brand is a deep, personal and continual relationship with a network of clients.

In fashion, the micro-brand is quickly becoming the preferred choice for people bored to death with corporate fashion. Now, a global network of small clothiers produce for a core set of clients and sell at private trunk shows or other events in key cities on a regular basis. Not only does the producer travel to the client, but the client waits to purchase a large quantity of clothes at one time, face-to-face with the producer. Often it is custom ordered, even through the web, because the clothier holds personal data such as sizing and color preferences. This trend provides great opportunity for entrepreneurs, especially women, who need to juggle family life with the desire to maintain and grow a professional business. In some ways this is another example of star culture (with the idea of the custom Valentino for the Academy Awards) working its way into hub culture.

But the micro-brand model works at many levels – from high-end private shows to designers who work in the developing world to create "authentic" fashions. One example is a woman in Bali who has developed traditional Indonesian batiks in Western styles for small hotel and other business-based lines. Her model was to employ people in Balinese villages with a simple set of tools, designs and instructions. In so doing, her micro-development initiative employed women and children in home-based industry, giving the undereducated a skill and saving them from the fate of many around them who were forced into Bali's growing sex industry. The growth of micro-initiatives like this one, especially when they are refined for a global urban audience, has many positive effects. There is some irony however – for though the net result is greatly positive for the villagers she works with, and she has been successful in the development of products the hub wants, large organizations such as the IMF and WTO, along with most protest organizations, would classify her use of children and teenagers in the program as illegal and immoral. In reality she is helping those communities, but on paper she violates the growing "ethical" principles of big business.

The Gated Universe: Hub People in Development

For the people who make up hub culture, the future is about reconciling brands on a personal level, (including the brand they call themselves) with their quest to reach that higher spiritual understanding.

The different aspects of hub people profiled in this book share a similar progression. From their motivators: travel and communication, to their key identity factors: work, relationships and leisure, they are looking for ways to connect their identity to something more permanent than materialism.

During that journey, they employ various cultural factors to get them by, including proximity, anonymity, culture adoption and biculturalism, reliance on word of mouth, experience addiction, and the acceptance and rejection of trends with studied ambivalence.

In the near future, the growth of spiritualism will be a leading factor in the cultural conversation of the hubs. One of the most interesting, but dangerous, aspects of this growth in spirituality will be the emergence of branded religion. With this emergence will come great power to the organizations that define the components of that experience, and with such power comes great danger.

The seeds of such a branded religion are around us in an infant state. The attempts of Scientology to create a religion that is "cool" have been very successful, but have left most people with a feeling that the organization is more about mind control than personal development. Poor branding.

Falun Gong is a Chinese-based meditation group, fringe religion or an evil cult, depending on whom you talk to. It has enjoyed amazingly fast growth in the development of its brand of religion by relying on very hub-esque principles – the use of guerilla organization tactics, digital communication and travel to organize itself. It is the only group in the history of China to "secretly" organize mass meditations in Tiananmen Square (reportedly up to 10,000 people at one time) behind the backs of Chinese authorities, prompting a swift but not very effective crackdown.

But these are nothing compared to the potential for a religion that found a way to combine multidimensional entertainment with the hub's quest for spiritualism. The building blocks of such a phenomenon are obvious: visually-led multimedia sermons of fast-paced presentations, a focus on acceptance, with non-confrontational material drawn from global sources (the Bible, Koran, Bhagavad Gita, and other ancient texts), and most importantly, a shift in timing. Instead of Sunday morning, such a religion would be most effective on Saturday night, when hub culture is out playing. Not on the street bugging people, but as a destination. Instead of making people get up early on Sunday morning, such an organization could more easily keep them up late, providing a meeting point during the ubiquitous Saturday night social scene. Most interestingly, it could even be done online, virtually, as persistent universe gaming becomes more common. Positioned as a spiritual service, such an organization would charge a flat fee, like a gym or a class, avoiding the guilt that comes with public collection of money in the modern church.

The concept becomes even more fascinating with the addition of more aspects of hub culture to the equation. What if it combined yoga and some form of sport and exercise to connect the mind and body? What if it provided a networking opportunity and a sense of status, like old churches used to be when they were the backbone of Western society, before their brands were made obsolete by the erosion of their influence in the financial and political worlds? What if everyone popped a Prozac before they went, or technology forbid, one of the new mood-enhancing drugs that replicate scratonin (the dopamine released by Ecstasy), now currently under clinical trial by big pharma, to connect the group on a level matched in raves and dance clubs? The implications are staggering. It is potentially positive, probably negative, certainly controversial and it is certainly coming.

The idea also skews toward the young. To most people over 30, such a religion seems quite foreign and "false," going against the construct of tradition. But in a culture where tradition is recycled, the idea makes sense, and the younger the targets, the more easy it will be to sell. For the young in hub culture, the thinking goes, if it works for me in building that connection to God, a higher self, et al., then it's worth a try. Especially if it is fun.

That potential bombshell aside, for today's existing brands the result is opportunity to add value and slow commoditization in their selling proposition. The emergence of hub culture has given birth to a new common group of desirable consumers with great spending power spread across all urban markets. The problem is, they are increasingly gated, closed to anything that is outside their own world. To crack into that world, brands must speak to these consumers through their motivators, in the language of their identities and within the context of their cultural factors.

Once successful in cracking into the group, the real work begins, and that is to create a belief that the brand is more than a proxy of material goods designed to fill their spiritual hole. Instead, we say that the brand is in tune with their spiritual self by trying to get to that same place or coming from that place. To do this effectively, the organization and the product must reflect those spiritual attributes – truth, honor, respect for life, love, a sense of connection between the mind and the body and the soul. All those things that make up our mental construct of what is good, even holy. And not just as an element – it has to be a true core of the organization, not an act. Does your company act responsibly in its consumption of resources? Does it treat employees with respect? Does it pollute? Does it kill animals, or … people?

An example of this lies in a hub guy named James, who announced that despite how cool Krups is (the German purveyor of beautiful high-quality kitchen appliances – juicers, etc.) he would never again buy a Krups product. This was because he had read that Krups, in 1905, had been the leading munitions supplier in Germany, and directly played a role in the buildup of the German war machine, helping to cause two world wars. He loves Krups products but the history of Krups revolts him.

"I know it was a hundred years ago. But if only they had at least changed the brand name, to show some sort of conscious break from that legacy, it would be a bit better," he said.

Tomorrow's versions of Krups are today's companies destroying the environment – big companies that cut down forests for newspapers, books and magazines, and probably the entire oil, mining and auto industries. This is why the idea of Segway (both the scooter and compostible engine) and Dean Kamen's New Hampshire company DEKA has so captured the popular imagination – it has the potential to not only stop destruction in an industry (transportation), but to reverse it with revolutionary technology. James can't wait to get one.

"I'd easily pay three times the going price – it's just the right thing." he said.

Ethical morality and absolute environmental protection are the watermarks for business survival, not just success, in the near present. Today, in the absolute present, success with the hubs is best found through service, and thus, giving experience to the consumer. Through experience, they glimpse the spiritual development of a brand, because experience and service are functions of the people in the organization, not the material product. Since only other humans can identify that need for a connection to the spiritual, only they can speak for the brand as it tries to convince the consumer it too, is spiritual.

As more people in hub culture seek enlightenment, the more they will become disenchanted with materialism. People will simply stop buying for the reasons that we try to sell to them now. If they stop buying, then the brand dies, and so with it the company. Branding must evolve with the people. More people, led by those in hub culture, are evolving, or at least trying to, toward something beyond materialism. If they find spiritual understanding, and the brands move with them, then all can be good.

If not, then we will all have to deal with the consequences of the true backlash that is out there: now it is pockets of aggression separated by passive ambivalence, but it could be followed by a combined war of destruction against the very idea of brands and the people who blithely consume them. It will be fought by those who have woken to the branding charade, but missed finding a spiritual connection to drive them forward; a group that realize not that they don't care, but that they have no hope. Fair warning? Namaste.

Hub Culture at a glance, a marketer's checklist:

Poles: travel, communication

Motivators: work, leisure, relationships

Cultural factors: proximity, anonymity, culture adoption, biculturalism, reliance on word of mouth, experience addiction, and the acceptance and disposal of trends with studied ambivalence

Target traits: environmentalism, purity of consumption (organic, sustainable), personalization, service and experience

Calculating the value of branding to a hub targeted good or service, ceteris paribus:

Q   : Quantity of goods in market

QL   : Quality relative to the market (decimal percentage relative to the Pc greater than 1)

S   : Scarcity relative to the market (decimal percentage relative to Q less than 1)

BV   : Brand Value

P   : Price

Pc   : commodity price

Pd   : derived value price

Pp   : price premium differential

Be   : brand equity

Bp   : brand premium

I   : Input, units of goods sold

■ **If your brand proposition is based on quality,**

$BV = P*QL$

Calculate the value of your good by multiplying the price by the Quality relative to the market. If the price is \$100 and your product is 20% better than the best product out there, the brand value is \$120.

■ **If your brand proposition is based on scarcity,**

$BV = Q/S$

Calculate the brand value of your good by dividing the quantity in a specified basket by the Scarcity relative to the market. If the quantity of units is 100 in a basket of goods, and your product is 3% more scarce (unique) than the other goods in the basket, the brand value of the good is 3% higher than comparable products.

■ To calculate the price premium differential,

$Pp = Pd - Pc$

Where the premium is the subtraction of the highest commodity price in the market from the derived value price you are able to charge. Derived value price is the highest price you are able to charge after all incentives and discounts are subtracted from the selling price.

■ To calculate realized net price premiums on branding investment,

$Bp = Pp*I/Be$

Where inputs are individual units of goods sold and derived value price minus commodity price is the price premium differential you are able to command in the market. Divide by Brand equity, the sum of invested value (advertising, PR, etc) to find the realized premium on branding investment for a good.

Index